THE INDIAN CEO

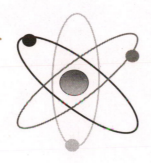

THE INDIAN CEO
A Portrait of Excellence

SIGNE M. SPENCER
THARUMA RAJAH
S.A. NARAYAN
SEETHARAMAN MOHAN
GAURAV LAHIRI

Response
Business books from SAGE
Los Angeles ■ London ■ New Delhi ■ Singapore
www.sagepublications.com

First published in 2007 by

Response Books
Business books from SAGE
B 1/I 1, Mohan Cooperative Industrial Area
Mathura Road, New Delhi 110 044

Sage Publications Inc
2455 Teller Road
Thousand Oaks, California 91320

Sage Publications Ltd
1 Oliver's Yard, 55 City Road
London EC1Y 1SP

Sage Publications Asia-Pacific Pte Ltd
33 Pekin Street
#02-01 Far East Square
Singapore 048763

Published by Vivek Mehra for Response Books, Laser typeset in 10.5/13 Trebuchet MS by Excellent Laser Typesetters, Delhi, and printed at Chaman Enterprises, New Delhi.

Tenth Printing 2008

Library of Congress Cataloging-in-Publication Data

The Indian CEO: a portrait of excellence / Signe M. Spencer ... [et al.].
      p. cm.
   1. Chief executive officers—India. 2. Leadership—India. I. Spencer, Signe M., 1950–

HD38.25.I4I53	658.4'20954—dc22	2007	2007001626

ISBN: 978-0-7619-3362-5 (PB)   978-81-7829-704-0 (INDIA-PB)
      978-0-7619-3361-8 (HB)   978-81-7829-818-4 (INDIA-HB)

The Sage Team: Leela Kirloskar, Anupama Purohit and Mathew P.J.

*Dedicated
to the cause of
management research
in India*

Contents

List of Tables

List of Figures

List of Boxes

Foreword

Distinguishing Outstanding Leaders

Competency-based human resource practices have gone from new techniques to common practice over the past 25 years. Major consulting companies, such as HayGroup, PDI, DDI, and Linkage have become worldwide practitioners in competency assessment and development, and conducted major international conferences, with competency validation studies conducted in over 100 countries. This work has focused on all types of occupations. Since most of this research is done by psychologists based in consulting companies, most of the studies remain unpublished, giving rise to an exaggerated perception in academic circles that there is a lack of empirical evidence on the topic. A brief review of the history of competency assessment will provide a context for the reader.

Milestones in the History of Competency Research

1958   David McClelland and colleagues Allen Baldwin, Urie Bronfenbrenner, and Fred Strodbeck publish *Talent and Society: New Perspectives in the Identification of Talent* (D. Van Nostrand, New Jersey). They frame the search for early identification of talent as a challenge to definition of talent and introduce the concept of abilities as more central than personality. Work, in the 1960s, on developing achievement motivation in India and other countries builds on this concept to develop behavioral aspects of talent.

1970   The first 'job competency assessment' study is con-
       ducted at McBer and Company for Supervisory Chap-
       lains in the US Navy by Richard Boyatzis. In the next
       few years, the early studies in the public and private
       sector used psychological tests as measures of the
       competencies. Early projects were conducted for the
       US Department of Human Services, US State Depart-
       ment, US Navy, General Electric, Wilkes Lumber and
       Furniture, DEC, DAYCO, and others.

1973   David McClelland attached the competency label to
       this emerging area of study when he published 'Test-
       ing for Competence Rather than Intelligence' in the
       American Psychologist. It blamed the testing and re-
       cruitment industries for misdirecting the quest for
       talent and challenged professionals to look for the
       'competencies' that really differentiated high perform-
       ing talent.

1975   The 'Behavioral Event Interview' was developed at
       McBer and Company as an interview version of the
       Thematic Apperception Test. It opened the door for
       inductive determination of competencies and used an
       extreme case design for validation.

1982   Richard Boyatzis published *The Competent Manager*
       (John Wiley & Sons, New York), the first empirical test
       showing that competencies determining outstanding
       managers and executives at all levels in public and
       private sector organizations predict effectiveness. It
       showed the first generic competency model of man-
       agement, the definition of a job competency and a
       model of personality based on McClelland's book, *Per-
       sonality* (Holt, Rinehart & Winston, New York), show-
       ing multiple levels of the competencies within the
       person.

1993   Lyle and Signe Spencer publish *Competence at Work*
       (John Wiley & Sons, New York). Using a conceptual

review of hundreds of competencies models, they developed generic models of managers, sales, R&D, HR
professionals, and entrepreneurs. They introduced the
concept of developmental levels within each competency.

1996   David McClelland proposed using tipping points to determine how much of a competency is sufficient for
outstanding performance. HayGroup uses this technique. McClelland makes the proposal in an article
published posthumously in 1998.

1998   Dan Goleman publishes *Working with Emotional Intelligence* (Bantam, New York). He reframes most of the
competencies in the generic models as emotional
intelligence.

2006   Richard Boyatzis publishes, in *Psicothema*, an empirical study of leaders in an international consulting company showing that tipping points results in better
prediction of financial performance.

2007   The present publication, the first empirical test of
Indian leadership competencies, showing which com-
petencies determine outstanding performance of
Indian CEOs.

The study of leadership has taken many twists and turns over
the decades, but one persistent theme is inquiry into the type
of person that is a great or effective leader. It is clear that
the essence of leadership is a relationship between the leader
and the people around him or her, which we call a resonant
relationship.[1] But, what is it that allows or enables a person
to initiate or sustain such a relationship?

Research published over the last 30 years or so shows us
that outstanding leaders appear to require three clusters of
talent as *threshold abilities* and five clusters of competencies as *distinguishing outstanding performance*. The three
threshold abilities are:

1. Expertise and experience is a threshold level of competency;
2. Knowledge (i.e. declarative, procedural, functional and meta-cognitive) is a threshold competency; and
3. An assortment of basic cognitive competencies, such as memory and deductive reasoning, are threshold competencies.

There are five clusters of competencies that *differentiate outstanding* from average performing leaders and managers in many countries of the world.[2] They are:

1. Cognitive competencies, such as systems thinking and pattern recognition;
2. Emotional intelligence competencies of self-awareness, such as emotional self-awareness;
3. Emotional intelligence competencies of self-management, such as emotional self-control, adaptability, and initiative;
4. Social intelligence competencies of social awareness, such as empathy; and
5. Social intelligence competencies of relationship management, such as developing others and teamwork.

Are competencies enough for outstanding performance? No. So, let us look at the larger picture for the role of competencies.

Beyond Competencies to A Broader View of Talent

Figure F.1 displays a basic contingency model of outstanding performance with the role of competencies, and is an enhancement of the model shown in Boyatzis' book, *The Competent Manager*. Beyond competencies, a person's talent can

Figure F.1: Theory of Action and Job Performance from
The Competent Manager
(Best Fit = Area of Maximum Stimulation, Challenge, and Performance)

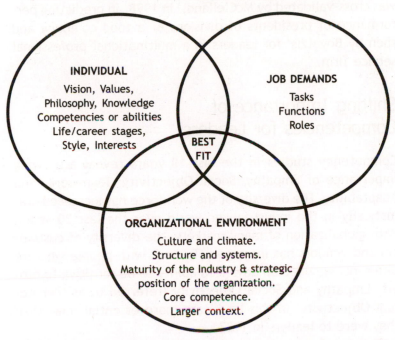

be said to include their values, vision, and philosophy, as well as their life and career stage that will affect their desire to use abilities they have shown in the past or develop new ones. The job demands affect performance directly through roles and task responsibilities. Components of the organizational environment that relate to competencies to stimulate maximum performance include the culture and climate, structure and systems, strategic position within the industry or sector, and core competence of the organization, more accurately these are the factors that relate to the clusters of competencies to create a best fit.

As suggested by Boyatzis, clusters of competencies appear to hold more promise in understanding the 'best fit' than merely single competencies. Using one or two competencies from each of the clusters is far more effective than using all the competencies in one of two clusters. This finding was cross-validated by McClelland,[3] in 1998, in predicting performance of presidents of divisions of a food company and then by Boyatzis[4] for leaders in a multinational professional service firm.

Shifting Importance of Competencies for Leaders

Competency studies in the last 10 years reveal a growing importance of Empathy, Social Objectivity, Teamwork, and Adaptability. The diversity of the workforce has increased dramatically in the industrialized world over the last 20 years. With globalization of many markets, the diversity of customers and vendors has increased. To work with people who are different, we need an advanced ability to be sensitive to others. Empathy and Social Objectivity (referred to as 'Perceptual Objectivity' in this book) are more essential now, than they were to leaders in 1982.

The use of teams has increased. Downsizing and de-layering organizations meant more interdependence on fewer people. To address customer needs and improve quality, multifunctional, project and self-managing teams were developed as essential work units. Working with others—across geographic distances, asynchronously with computer-based systems—has provoked the need for more sophisticated skills in working with others. All of these factors have propelled the teamwork competency to primary importance in managing and leading today.

The myriad changes in our society and work, and even the increase in the rate of change, conspire to make life less certain. It inspires a belief that the future, even the near future, will be dramatically different than the present. It is no wonder that Adaptability and the ability to tolerate uncertainty have also become essential competencies in guiding others.

Tipping Points for Outstanding Leaders

A major advancement in understanding the effect of competencies on performance came from catastrophe theory, which is now considered a subset of complexity theory. Instead of asking only the typical question, 'Which competencies are needed or necessary for outstanding performance?' David McClelland, in a paper published posthumously in 1998, posed the question, 'How often do you need to show a competency to 'tip' you into outstanding performance? In other words, how frequently should a competency be shown to be sufficient for maximum performance? He reported that the presidents of the divisions of a large food company, using competencies above the tipping points, received significantly higher bonuses, which were proportional to the profitability of their divisions, as compared to their less profitable peers.

Using this method, Boyatzis replicated, in 2006, significant findings regarding tipping points in an international consulting firm. The profits from accounts of senior partners were analyzed for seven quarters following assessment of their competencies. Senior partners using competencies above the tipping point more than doubled the operating profits from their accounts as compared to the senior partners below the tipping point. The measure of competencies was the average perceived frequency of use of each competency by others around the senior partner, using a 360 degree competency questionnaire. He showed that this method was superior to a simple median split or continuous analysis of the relationship between the frequency of competencies shown and financial performance of the senior partners, leaders, of this firm.

Knowing the point at which a person's use of a competency tips him/her into outstanding performance provides vital guidance to managers and leaders. It helps those coaching others know which competencies are the closest to added value in stimulating outstanding performance. The tipping point is sometimes referred to as a trigger point.

The tipping point for each competency would be a function of the organization environment. For example, the manager of an office of a strategy consulting company would have a tipping point of Adaptability at the maximum level. To show sufficient Adaptability to be outstanding, (s)he would have to be using it 'frequently and consistently.' Their business, projects, and clients change each year. They typically have high turnover in consulting staff as well. Meanwhile, the manager of a basic chemical processing plant may have a tipping point of only 'occasional or often' of Adaptability. The certainty of their product line and predictability of their production processes does not create as much uncertainty as the consulting business. They probably have low turnover in the chemical plant as well, requiring even less adaptation to new staff. Analysis of tipping points should become a standard feature of competency assessment studies in the future.

Competencies can be Developed

Although the understanding of competencies themselves has been extended, perhaps the most important contributions in the last 30 years have come about primarily in the last 15 years. Despite the 'honeymoon effect' of typical training programs, that might start with improvement immediately following the program, but within months it drops precipitously. Only 15 programs were found in a global search of the literature by the Consortium on Research on Emotional Intelligence in Organizations to improve emotional intelligence. Most of them showed an impact on job outcomes, such as number of new businesses started, or life outcomes, such as finding a job or satisfaction,[5] which are the ultimate purpose of development efforts. But showing an impact on outcomes, though desired, may blur *how* the change actually occurs. Furthermore, when a change has been noted, a question is raised about the sustainability of the change because of the relatively short time periods of the study. It provides hope that people can develop competencies, but it all starts with knowing which competencies are most important in determining outstanding and effective performance.

Concluding Thought

Competencies are a critical ingredient to outstanding performance. Although our understanding of competencies has expanded dramatically in the last 30 years, the most inspiring insights have come from research showing we can develop these competencies. Adults can develop competencies so vital to outstanding performance in management, leadership, and many other occupations and professions. As leaders and managers, we can only create environments in which others want to use their capabilities and competencies if we are authentic and consistent in our own demonstration of these behaviors. Through the intentional change process, we have the opportunity to truly make a difference. Whether applied in universities or companies, government agencies or not-for-profits, this process can help us coach each other to create the social environments we want and find so conducive to making a difference. The study you are about to read adds a tremendous amount of data-based insight to this discussion and will guide the development of leaders in India and other countries for years. Enjoy the adventure you are about to begin!

~ **Richard E. Boyatzis, PhD**
Professor, Case Western Reserve University

Notes

1. R. Boyatzis and A. McKee (2005), '*Resonant Leadership: Renewing Yourself and Connecting With Others Through Mindfulness, Hope, and Compassion*', Harvard Business School Press, Boston; and D. Goleman, R. Boyatzis, and A. McKee (2002), *Primal Leadership: Realizing the Power of Emotional Intelligence*, Harvard Business School Press, Boston.

2. D.W. Bray, R.J. Campbell, and D.L. Grant (1974), *Formative years in business: A Long Term AT&T Study of Managerial Lives*, John Wiley & Sons, New York; R.E. Boyatzis (1982), *The Competent Manager: A Model for Effective Performance*, John Wiley & Sons, New York; F. Luthans, R.M. Hodgetts, and S.A. Rosenkrantz (1988), *Real Managers*, Ballinger Press, Cambridge; G.C. Thornton III and W.C. Byham (1982), *Assessment Centers and Managerial Performance*, Academic Press, New York; A. Howard, and D. Bray (1988), *Managerial Lives in Transition: Advancing Age and Changing Times* Guilford Press, New York; J.P. Kotter (1982), *The General Managers*, Free Press, New York; J.P. Kotter (1988), *The Leadership Factor*, Free Press, New York; J.P. Campbell, M.D. Dunnette, E.E. Lawler III, and K.E. Weick (1970), *Managerial Behavior, Performance, and Effectiveness*, McGraw Hill, New York.

3. D.C. McClelland (1998), 'Identifying competencies with behavioral event interviews', *Psychological Science* Vol. 9(5), pp. 331-39.

4. R.E. Boyatzis (2006), 'Using tipping points of emotional intelligence and cognitive competencies to predict financial performance of leaders', *Psicothema*, Vol. 18, pp. 124-31.

5. C. Cherniss and M. Adler (2000), 'Promoting emotional intelligence in organizations: Make training in emotional intelligence effective', American Society of Training and Development, Washington D.C.

Acknowledgements

This book could not have been possible without the devotion and dedication of many people who care deeply about the future development and growth of India's economy. This work was inspired and sponsored by The Public Enterprises Selection Board (PESB), led by T.K.A. Nair, and Bharat Petroleum Corporation Limited (BPCL), without whose active, committed and practical support this study couldn't have been produced.

The Research team worked long and hard, collecting interviews and background materials, reading, coding and analyzing the data. It consisted of Cheryl Chow, Mark Iob, Micheal Jensen and Hima Vagani (from the HayGroup), plus Rajorshi Ganguli and Krishnan (of BPCL), without whose dedication this study would not have been possible.

We would also sincerely like to thank all the Ministers, the CEOs who generously gave their time and frank descriptions of their experiences; the members of the steering and validating committees, for taking out time from their busy schedules to contribute to and validate the research.

Our sincere thanks to Dr. Manmohan Singh for his valuable inputs for the Study when he was the Leader of the Opposition in the Parliament. We express our gratitude for his guidance as well as participation in the subsequent discussions leading to the launch of the Study by him as the Prime Minister of India.

We also express our gratitude to:

M.S. Banga (Unilever), Sarthak Behuria (CMD, IOC), Subodh Bhargava (Ex CII, Eicher), R.S.S.L.N. Bhaskarudu (Former Chairman, PESB), R.P. Billimoria (Billimoria Consultants),

Kumar Mangalam Birla (Aditya Birla Group), D.S. Brar (Ex Ranbaxy), M.N. Buch (Ex PESB), B.C. Bora (Former CMD ONGC), James Burruss (HayGroup), Keki Dadiseth (Unilever), Xerxes Desai (Former MD, Titan), Y.C. Deveshwar (ITC), Govind Ethiraj (CNBC), George Fernandes (Former Minister of Defence), Mary Fontaine (HayGroup), H.C. Gandhi (Ex PESB), Pankaj Ghemawat (Harvard Business School), Dr. Pradipto Ghosh (Ex Prime Minister's Office), D.V. Gupta (Ex AAI), Indrajit Gupta (Business World), Dr. Richard Hackman (Harvard Business School), Dr. Abid Hussain (JNU), Dr. J.J. Irani (Tata Sons), C.P. Jain (NTPC), Arun Jaitley (Former Minister of Law), Dr. A.H. Kalro (IIMK), K.V. Kamath (ICICI), Dr. Kanan (IOC), Ravi Kant (Tata Motors), V.N. Kaul (Comptroller and Auditor General of India), Dr. Vijay Kelkar (Advisor to Finance Minister), P.N. Khandwala (Ex IIMA), Dr. Rakesh Khurana (Harvard Business School), Dr. V.K. Koshy (Bharat Electronics Limited), M.B. Lal (HPCL), Dr. Paul Lawrence (Harvard Business School), Yash Mahajan (Punjab Tractors), Keshub Mahindra (M&M), Ravi Marwaha (IBM), Amit Mitra (FICCI), Chandra Mohan (21st Century Batteries), Dato' Azman Mokhtar (MD of Khazanah Holdings, Malaysia), Dr. K.R.S. Murthy (Ex IIM), N.R. Narayan Murthy (Infosys), A.M. Naik (L&T), Ram Naik (Former Minister of Petroleum), Naresh Narad (Secretary, Government of India), Aditya Narayan (ICI), Dr. Nitin Nohria (Harvard Business School), Arvind Pande (Former CMD, SAIL), Deepak Parekh (HDFC), Ashok Parthasarthy, M.A. Pathan (Former CMD, IOC), Raji Philip (Hindustan Paper Corporation Limited), Suresh Prabhu (Member of Parliament), C.R. Prasad (Former CMD, GAIL), Y. Prasad (National Hydroelectric Power Corporation), Subir Raha (Former CMD, ONGC), K.G. Ramachandran (BHEL), M.S. Ramachandran (IOC), Ramanathan (IPCL), Late Dr. Raja Ramanna (MP, Rajya Sabha), V. Kasturi Rangan (Harvard Business School), Jerry Rao (Mphasis), Dr. A. Sahay (Scooters India Limited), Sudensha Sen (Economic Times), Arun

Shourie (Former Minister of Disinvestment and Telecom), Dr. Madhukar Shukla (XLRI), Rajendra Singh (Ex NTPC), R.P. Singh (Power Grid Corporation), P.M. Sinha (Former CEO Pepsi India), South Asian Business School Association at Harvard Business School, P.K. Srivastav (Shipping Corporation of India), Dr. Phil Stone (Harvard), U. Sundararajan (Ex BPCL), Dr. Vardharajan (Member of Parliament), K. Cherian Varghese (Corporation Bank), D.K. Varma (Rashtriya Chemicals and Fertilizers), and A.C. Wadhawan (Ex PESB).

T.K.A. Nair, former Chairman, PESB and presently Principal Secretary to the Prime Minister of India, also gave his valuable time. His guidance has been of immense value in bringing out this publication.

We would like to thank the people who provided support, feedback and review of the book as it was being written: Vertika Verma (HayGroup) who guided the manuscript through its many phases, Deb Nunes and Kirsta Anderson (HayGroup), Dr. Phil Stone (Harvard University) and Jocelyn Anthony.

Preface

The Purpose of this Book

In India, today, there has been a lack of contemporary research in studying the intrinsic attributes (like the need to achieve) that leaders of large enterprises use in leading their organizations to success. If we can discover Indian leadership behaviors and characteristics that are highly effective today, then it will be possible to develop many more leaders who will make India competitive, and accelerate her path to economic development.

This book details the results of the original empirical research on the behaviors and thoughts used by the outstanding Indian leaders to obtain their results—not just theories and opinions or self reports. It gives the readers a portrait of the CEOs and CMDs of India's most outstanding companies at the turn of the millennium. With the generous participation of a sample of these outstanding CEOs in India, HayGroup identified some of the most important leadership competencies and behaviors that have enabled them to lead their companies to achieve outstanding results. However, we will not describe their personal backgrounds, families, career histories, religion, or philosophies of leadership—except when these factors directly impact the decisions and behaviors that enable them to achieve outstanding results in leading their companies.

The original intention of this study was to

- provide tools for the Public Enterprises Selection Board (PESB) to improve both their own and their companies' performance by matching leaders to companies even more accurately than they had been doing.

The findings of this study would help not only in developing and training the existing leaders to become more successful, but also in developing future leaders and benchmarking their skill-sets, strategies, and successes in order to ensure the attainment of the India 2020 vision. This study should be helpful to different groups of people:

- For current CEOs/CMDs: providing 'food for thought' regarding their role and their own competency development; providing reminders or suggestions on which leadership behaviors have been most effective in various scenarios;
- For current business leaders and aspiring CEOs, and for the mentors and teachers of aspiring CEOs: providing a model of competencies they may wish or need to develop, and, we hope, examples and ideas that will provoke thought and inspire action.
- For academics: examples and ideas that will stimulate discussion and, we hope, further research; and perhaps provide material to further enrich the education of the next generation of business leaders.
- For business students: a model of excellence today and perhaps a peek into the future.
- For the general reader: who has a big appetite and wants to learn and expand his own skill-sets after reading about the best leaders in India.

India needs to build a new generation of leaders who, along with their capabilities and a business friendly environment, are determined to make a positive contribution to the business by unleashing the human capital to be creative and innovative. A quote in the book *India 2020: A Vision for the New Millennium* says that

Somehow over the years, we have developed a habit of giving low priority to actual action on the ground. People may ask why we think there will be action now, when earlier there was a relative slack. The answer, we believe, lies in appreciating that a large part of our population is young and raring for change. This has unleashed a large amount of entrepreneurial talent and adventurous spirit in India.

How it all Started

Through his years of experience in dealing with Public Sector Enterprises (PSEs) of different kinds both at the state level as well as at the national level, T.K.A. Nair, former Chairman of the Public Enterprises Selection Board (PESB), knew that a PSE needed a CEO with skill-sets depending on the organization's level of performance. He knew that the person who could lead a *Navratna*—a status accorded by the Government of India to nine of the leading Public Sector Companies in India—would be very different from the kind of person who could turn around an ailing company. He also believed that the best talent in the public sector would obviously prefer to work for the profit making PSEs rather than the 'Sick and Wounded' or 'In a state of Coma' PSEs.

What Nair was looking for was, in effect, a far more focused selection process for the CEOs that would help each public sector organization in India to identify and bring out the best suited leader. He was looking for more efficient ways of selecting the CEO for each of the PSEs, based on its unique requirement and not an arbitrary one size-fits-all selection process.

Early in 2000, the inevitable happened—the three stage reforms process in the oil and gas sector finally culminated in dismantling of the administered price mechanism (APM). This third stage of deregulation in the oil and gas sector was to expose all public sector oil companies to the competition, both local and global. There were concerns within Bharat Petroleum Corporation Limited (BPCL) too. Being a PSE itself, BPCL in recent times had not faced the travails of competitive pressures. However, the realization was seeping in that with the multinationals entering the market, its market position would be in jeopardy, and it was just a matter of time before it actually happened. Immediate actions were needed to survive the process of deregulation.

The first task that BPCL CEO, Sundararajan undertook was re-organizing the company, basically transforming it into a customer-centric organization, where primacy of the customer would be respected at all times. According to his Director (HR), S.A. Narayan, the Territory Manager's role was very critical when it came to engaging with the customer. So he commissioned HayGroup to undertake Competency Modeling for the Territory Managers. The consulting firm created the competency model after extensive research comparing the outstanding with average managers and finally validating the finding of the study through a group of Senior Managers.

At one such communication session, where the model was being presented to the Territory Managers, Narayan invited Nair to join. He was impressed with the fact that such a contextual model could be developed where the competencies of the managers could be defined in terms of observed behavior. In turn, it could enhance their development process by leaps and bounds and could be used as an effective tool for assessing their suitability for various assignments. He was enthused by the study since he felt that it enabled a correct match of an individual with the job. As he was on the look out for a more efficient selection procedure for CEOs in PSEs, Narayan invited him to attend BPCL's 'Train the Trainer' workshop in Delhi. At this workshop, Senior BPCL Managers were being trained on the Behavioral Event Interview (BEI) technique, so that the selection of Territory Managers could be based on the individual's underlying competencies as opposed to mere knowledge and experience alone.

During the workshop, Nair, Narayan and Director of HayGroup, Tharuma Rajah, deliberated and discussed the performance of the Public Sector Enterprises in India. The PSEs in India numbering over 200 were operating on a continuum of performance ranging from 'Start-ups' to 'Turnarounds' to 'Sick and Wounded' or 'In a state of Coma.'

Since BPCL, in association with HayGroup, had done empirical research to determine the process and standards for selecting its Territory Managers, Nair thought on the lines of conducting a similar study for the PESB. But this time, the scope of the study would be much more critical to make the selection process of CEOs more robust and effective. He discussed with Rajah the possibility of conducting a similar study aimed at deciphering the competencies of outstanding CEOs in the public sector and develop a Competency Model. For Rajah, this was an opportunity to work in India, something he had longed for, and an opportunity he would not let pass.

HayGroup had previously carried out a similar study on Global Leadership where CEOs from all over the world had participated but this new study would focus specifically on the CEOs from India. Surely, it was a challenging task as it would require a thorough research process and consultations with a cross section of stakeholders including past and present CEOs, senior government officials and members of the media as well as academicians. But being a landmark project that this was, HayGroup decided to use the best possible consultants from its global network for formulating the study and ensuring its credibility. This was an opportunity to augment the performance of Public sector in India by having a better selection procedure for CEOs and Sundararajan, being the visionary leader that he was, saw this as an opportunity to make a contribution to the Indian Public Sector. He agreed to offer the support of the BPC officers and also fund the Project.

The two day workshop ended with not only a group of professionals trained in advanced selection techniques, but also with three people committed to forming a triad that would conduct the first ever leadership study for the Public Sector in India. Nair would provide leadership and direction to the study; Sundararajan would secure funding and ensure logistical support and Rajah would assemble a world-class team from the Hay Global network to conduct the study. Thus, the stage was set for this important research study.

The Route Map

There is a sequential road map that this book follows. It focuses on the **personal characteristics** of the best Indian CEOs which when applied in the appropriate **situations,** enabled them to get outstanding results. The **situations** are examined at several levels of detail, ranging from a general Indian business context to specific business scenarios.

- *Chapter 1:* Here we look at the current business situation and the special challenges Indian CEOs face in executing their great ideas.
- *Chapter 2:* This chapter gives a brief overview of the HayGroup and David McClelland; focusing on his research in India. It also gives a brief overview of the research methodology used in this study.
- *Chapter 3:* The 'CEO Model' is discussed here along with an overview of the competencies and clusters.
- *Chapter 4:* A case study from an interview which illustrates upfront how different behaviors and competencies can fit together to produce results. This provides a sample of the kind of data and analysis used.
- *Chapter 5-8:* These chapters present each of the clusters and the competencies in that cluster in detail. The competencies are described upfront and supported with examples for enhancing the reader's understanding as well as the various development levels for the competency.
- *Chapter 9-12:* In these chapters we look at three common scenarios, representing three different business

situations: Turnarounds, Start-ups and Improving a Steady State; plus one common task (Boundary Management). We examine what leaders do to get the best results in each scenario. This is illustrated with short examples from the interviews, which show how the competencies support outstanding results in these business scenarios.

- *Chapter 13:* We look at the competencies of the leaders in the context of differences between the public sector enterprises versus those in the private sector, as well as contrasting competencies shown in the Indian situation with those seen in an international comparison group.
- *Chapter 14:* This chapter conveys some suggestions for ways to make the overall Indian context more enabling of business success and economic growth.

A Caution for the Reader

Don't read this book as setting limits to what you—or your leaders—might or should do. This book describes the consistent characteristics and behaviors of the best Indian CEOs at this time. It provides a picture of the **key** things that Indian leaders do, and are doing in order to create socially responsible business excellence now. However, there are also other things that great Indian leaders do today (just not as consistently)— and surely there will be even more as India develops and her business becomes more integrated into the global economy. So, use this book as a starting point—but not as a limit.

Note

1. The Private Sector calls its leaders as CEOs, while the Public Sector uses the term CMDs. In this book, the terms CEO and CMD are used inter-changeably. When referring to the Public Sector only the term CMD is used, Whereas CEO is used while referring to both the Private Sector and the Public Sector.

1 Indian Leaders: Challenges in Execution

The HayGroup office in Gurgaon (India) overlooks the half-constructed flyover marring the otherwise liberal expanse of National Highway No. 8. It is in about the same state since we started our work four years ago. In stark contrast, when we travel to China we see cars zipping past places where the very foundations were being laid only three months ago!

So does this mean that Indian workers are less capable than Chinese workers? One would think not. Indian workers in Dubai are building one floor a day, while those in Delhi take as many as two months to accomplish the same. Apparently the problem has little to do with Indian workers per se.

Then, is it the Indian leaders? Academicians, media professionals, CEOs and officials in the government—all those who helped us prepare this research seem to think so. They agree—almost unanimously—that the problem is 'great thinking but little execution'. Yet, Indians across the globe are making top-notch talent in many a field and fast becoming a force to reckon with. For example, demonstrating corporate leadership are L.N. Mittal, Chairman of the global steel company Arcelor Mittal; Arun Sarin, Chief Executive of the global mobile telecommunications company Vodafone; and Indra Nooyi, CEO of the global soft drink giant PepsiCo. Leading the academic frontier are Nitin Noria, Rakesh Kurana, C.K. Prahalad and Ram Charan. In the field of media are Kiran Desai, the 2006 Man Booker Prize winner; and Mira Nair, the Academy Award nominee. While these Indians, being emigrants, had the extra onus of adapting to a different culture and ethos, they, at the same time, proved to be exceptionally good at execution.

Our research was originally intended to address a different question:

> 'Looking at the best Indian corporate leaders—those who have, in fact, been successful at execution in India—*how* did they do it? What are the attitudes, the thoughts, behaviours and other characteristics that enabled them to be successful at execution?'

However, in the process of gathering data, we were confronted by two groups of factors that contributed to the much-discussed lack of execution—despite their impressive intelligence, competence and dedication—of the outstanding Indian CEOs we studied.[1]

Emotional Intelligence, Not just IQ

The first factor is grounded in two outstanding strengths of Indian leaders: their well-developed intellect and their competitive focus on achievement. Outstanding Indian CEOs stand head and shoulders above their peers in other countries, when it comes to their ability to think both analytically and strategically. In addition, they display a single-minded focus on growth in various forms. In this (as well as in terms of their inner strength), the finest Indian CEOs stand above their international counterparts and offer a model that their Western counterparts might do well to emulate. In many ways, these qualities are admirable and have led to the incredible growth and success in their businesses, while they have enabled some of the best Indian corporate leaders achieve substantial effectiveness in execution. But such admirable traits, when over-used or relied on too much, can carry a cost or become counter-productive.[2] The very success that is achieved by using these approaches also makes it difficult to broaden one's repertoire. This is more so when both the culture and the educational system have placed a great deal of emphasis and value on those same strengths. While we give far more importance on individual achievements [as exemplified by admission criteria for the country's finest academic institutions, the Indian Institutes of Technology Management (IITs/IIMs)], we give far less emphasis to contributing as part of a larger team—which, in order to be most effective, calls for an understanding of team members' individual capabilities and behaviors. Even the Indian national sport of cricket relies more on an accumulation of individual performances, rather than on an integrated and intricately coordinated interaction among players (such as is seen in soccer or basketball teams, or even jazz groups).

In the case of Indian business leaders, there is a dark side to their strongly developed intellects and achievement drives— a relative absence of *tuning in* to other people. In fact, at times they are so focused on entrepreneurship and strategy that they neglect the task of energizing their teams. However, when they *do* energize their teams, they get much better results; particularly when launching a new product or venture or building the capability of the organization itself (as we shall discuss in Chapters 6, 10, and 11).

More striking, however, is their lack of attention to others, especially as individuals—one on one. While Indian CEOs showed empathy and compassionate responses to entire groups or classes of people (part of what we call 'executive maturity'), the missing piece was a discernment of the *individual characteristics of the people closest to the leaders*. This crucial aspect of Emotional Intelligence is variously known as Inter-personal Understanding, Empathy, Good Judgement of People, or Tuning into Others. It is an ability to accurately recognize the others' *individual* behavioral strengths and limits, their interests or aspirations and the reasons behind their resistance to change. Though it may seem counter-intuitive, this quality is a great asset when it comes to effective and expeditious implementation. This was found in the International CEO study, where 'Good Judgement of People' was a key factor in implementation (see Appendix). This quality is consistently found in our own studies on leadership. A recent study in a multinational corporation showed that leaders who excelled in tuning in to people as individuals (and also showed two or three out of four closely-related competencies) produced an average revenue growth of 12 percent a year, over four years—as compared to their peers who lacked these characteristics and who lost an average of 8 percent revenue per year, in the same time frame and within the same company.[3] This is such a foundational competency that it is displayed consistently in the behavioral event interviews of CEOs and senior executives (more than three-quarters of outstanding CEOs and outstanding senior executives and over two-thirds of the 'average' CEOs). In stark contrast, only about one-eighth of outstanding Indian leaders demonstrated tuning in to others in their interviews. (We are *not* saying that Indian leaders demonstrated poor judgement of people, only that they simply overlooked this competency). This outstanding group of Indian leaders has nevertheless been highly successful. However, as their organizations become more complex and as international competition increases, we foresee that Indian CEOs will increasingly need to balance their formidable intellect and entrepreneurial energy with the ability to accomplish results through others, by motivating, inspiring and effectively deploying them to execute and implement the organization's strategies and plans.[4]

Why is this competency important for execution and implementation? There are two reasons: first, tuning in to others
allows leaders to deploy their resources more intelligently.
They can match the skills and motivations of individuals to
the needs of a particular situation with greater accuracy, and
they can compose teams that will work effectively together.
They can deploy their talent in a game of chess (taking individual capabilities and limits into account) rather than of
checkers (where the pieces are treated as essentially inter-
changeable). They can also provide advice, feedback and challenging assignments that greatly increase the capabilities of
their people. Beside all this, tuning in to others greatly en-
hances the leaders' ability to influence others—by addressing
their personal concerns, resistances and motivations. This
enables the leaders to get genuine commitment to their program, so that people execute with enthusiasm and energy.[5]
When leaders at all organizational levels use this form of
emotional intelligence, they enable the organization to at-
tract and retain the best employees. This will increasingly
become a competitive advantage as talent-hungry companies
from the rest of the world look to India for well-educated
young people, and as the demand for talent within India also
increases. Tuning in to people is equally useful in dealing with
stakeholders outside the organization—whether customers,
suppliers, potential partners or other parties such as media,
government officials and so on.

The Indian CEOs' need, as a group, to shift from strongly
entrepreneurial energy to a more balanced style of leadership
is parallel to that experienced in many rapidly growing organizations. The entrepreneurial founder may not be the best
leader of a much larger and more mature organization. The wiser
entrepreneurs have found a way to pass the baton to a new
generation of leaders. These leaders of the new, larger and more
complex organizations know that their primary job is to *create
the conditions in which other people can execute effectively.*[6]

Boundary Management and Environmental Constraints

In preparing this study, we heard much discussion about the constraints on the PSEs, about how much more time they spend on dealing with the various Ministries, regulators, and other government authorities, including answering Parliamentary and media questions, and so on, (i.e. 'boundary management') as compared to the heads of private enterprises. And we heard about how much better the environment is for business than it was years ago, before liberalization. We have no doubt that all of that is true. However, coming to this project with years of experience in studying and working with CEOs and senior leaders, and with a database of thousands of executive interviews, we were shocked by how boundary management absorbs so much attention and energy from the private sector as well as the public sector. The differences in issues of boundary management between the public and the private sector and between the past and the present are real, but they are dwarfed by the differences between the difficulties faced by even the private sector today in India and those faced by their counterparts (and, increasingly, their competitors) in the rest of the world.

In the behavioral event interview,[7] we ask the leader to tell us three or four stories about important recent events in their work life, where we can see *how* they go about getting results. We ask participants to alternate between high points (successes) and times when it was more difficult or frustrating or when, despite their best efforts they did not achieve the results they wanted. Other than that, participants have a free choice about what stories to tell, and we take their choices as reflecting what seems important or salient to them, what claims the most of their attention (though not necessarily of their actual time). Almost half of our participants provided a full story of their difficulties with government and regulators in this study. Public and private enterprise were equal in this respect. This does not count those participants who mentioned the problem but did not tell a full story about it. In contrast, *none* of an equal-sized sample of international CEOs told a story about boundary management as it is experienced here in India, and fewer than 1 percent of our sample of over 2,000 outstanding senior executives tell stories that even remotely relate to boundary management. Although executives in the West often complain about what they see as excessive regulation (for example, the Sarbanes-Oxley requirements in the US), their visceral and practical experience is quite different from what we heard in India.[8] We happened to interview a senior executive who was specifically charged with changing the organization to meet the new standards after Sarbanes-Oxley was passed. It would seem that if anyone in a private enterprise in the West would experience boundary management issues, it would be a leader in this role, in the first year after Sarbanes-Oxley. But, this was not the case. This leader's focus during that year was not primarily on Washington, responding to congressional inquiries, nor fending off media intrusions, as a leader in India might imagine. Instead, this leader spoke about choosing, organizing and inspiring the team; leading them to design new processes; and about coaching and developing subordinates to prepare them to take on larger leadership roles in other parts of the company. These stories were full of tuning in to individuals, and the project was executed satisfactorily, 'on time, and under budget'. The contrast to the painful experiences of the Indian CEOs in boundary management could not be greater.

The fact is that even the private enterprise CEOs in India experience a difficulty in boundary management that is, frankly, stunning in contrast to other parts of the world. This suggests that public ownership versus disinvestment is *not* the fundamental issue in the problem of boundary management. There are other countries, like Canada, Malaysia,

Singapore, France and New Zealand, where publicly owned companies operate on an efficient and competitive basis, without major boundary management issues. The fundamental issue here has to do partly with the sheer number and intricacy of governmental constraints and inspections and even more with the lack of clarity, timeliness and predictability in getting permission or license to do anything, and the lack of consistency and timeliness in the enforcement of existing laws.[9] The procedures and standards are often unclear, or are inconsistently interpreted, leading to un-manageable delays in getting things accomplished. This lack of clarity and predictability leads into difficulties with planning and execution, all the more so as businesses become larger and more complex. In addition, both politicians and the media feel free to ask intrusive questions and absorb significant amounts of business people's time in preparing detailed explanations. The problems with physical and social infrastructure reflect and intensify the uncertainties associated with government licenses. Roads, water, telephone lines, electricity, transportation and communication: all face deficits and inconsistent performance that impede timely execution. All these delays and uncertainties not only add to the cost of implementation and discourage foreign capital investment but also dissipate the energy and enthusiasm needed to maintain interest in execution. As such experiences are repeated over time, in personal life as well as at work, it takes extraordinary resilience to continue the struggle to implement anything. We did see truly extraordinary resilience, maturity and determination among these outstanding CEOs.

Hope for the Future

Nevertheless, there is hope and a new vision for India, Inc. These problems are not destiny: emotional intelligence can be learned, and already great progress has been made in improving the business environment and infrastructure in India. The very existence of this study and the undivided support and credence given by all sections of the Indian political spectrum and by prominent Indian business leaders, both past and present, ranging from the brick and mortar industries to the click and mortar industries as well as academics and media, demonstrates deep and broad commitment to developing a way forward for India. Further, the findings of this study show how the best Indian corporate leaders do execute effectively in challenging situations (Chapters 9–12), and the underlying competencies that enable them to do so (Chapters 5–8). It is our hope that this book will help many Indians to understand and emulate these excellent role models.

Notes

1. See D.C. McClelland (1973). 'Testing for Competence Rather Than for Intelligence', *American Psychologist*, 28, pp. 1–14.
2. For an account of this phenomenon in the West, see the article by Scott W. Spreier, Mary H. Fontaine, and Ruth L. Malloy, 'Leadership Run Amok', published in *Harvard Business Review*, June 2006, and available at www.HayGroup.com.
3. Proprietary, client-specific research conducted by the HayGroup McClelland Center, Boston, USA.
4. For more details on the value and impact of both empathy and executive maturity (which the best Indian CEOs display in abundance), see R.E. Boyatzis and A. McKee (2005). *Resonant Leadership: Renewing Yourself and Connecting With Others Through Mindfulness, Hope, and Compassion*, Boston, Harvard Business School Press; or see D. Goleman, R. Boyatzis, and A. McKee (2002). *Primal Leadership: Realizing the Power of Emotional Intelligence*, Harvard Business School Press, Boston. See also *Social Intelligence*, by Daniel P. Goleman, Bantam Publishers, New York, 2006.
5. The lack of tuning into others causes problems in the West as well. We have often observed this, and it is cited by Ram Charan and Geoffrey Colvin as the leading reason for 'failures' by American CEOs in 'Why CEOs Fail', published by *Fortune* magazine, June 21, 1999, as well as by other business researchers and writers, including Daniel Goleman and Richard Boyatzis (see earlier citations in this chapter).

6. For more details on how to create such conditions for an effective team see J. Richard Hackman's book, *Leading Teams: Creating the Conditions for Team Success*, Harvard Business School Press, Boston, 2002. In addition, Richard Hackman, et al, have a book forthcoming in 2007 (also from Harvard Business School Press) specifically about effective top teams (CEOs or Business Unit heads and their direct reports).

7. The behavioral event interview is a special interviewing technique developed by David McClelland. For more details of this method see Chapter 2 of this book, or see Lyle M. Spencer and Signe Spencer (1993), *Competence at Work*, John Wiley, New York.

8. For a detailed and inspiring account of how one American company dealt with this situation, see Eric M. Pillmore (2003), 'How We're Fixing Up Tyco', *Harvard Business Review*, Cambridge, MA, December.

9. This issue is discussed in some depth, along with an Indian model for technologically enabled change in this respect, in Chapter 5 of C.K. Prahalad's (2005) book *The Fortune at the Bottom of the Pyramid*, Wharton School Publishing.

2 | Research Methods

Mapping and building a model of India's leadership competency is a complex task. The country, with its human capital, is attracting financial resources on the basis of quality manpower, cost effectiveness, its English-speaking abilities, and a huge middle class. To be able to harness this advantage and build on it, leadership competencies have to match global expectations.

We, at Bharat Petroleum and the HayGroup, made the competency research methods developed by McClelland,[1] Boyatzis[2] and others[3] a starting point for building leadership competency modelling for India. The reasons for the choice were twofold. First, McClelland's methods have become the international best practice in studying leadership at the HayGroup and elsewhere.[4] Second, the underlying principles of his approach have made it especially appropriate to study Indian leadership in its own context (as discussed hereafter).

DAVID C. MCCLELLAND

David Clarence McClelland (1917–98), Professor of Psychology at the Harvard University, was the founder of McBer and Company (a part of the HayGroup now). Though McClelland is chiefly known for his work on achievement motivation—examining the relationship between intrinsic motivation and economic achievement (*The Achieving Society,* 1976)—his research interests extended to personality and consciousness. His theories promoted improvements in employee assessment methods, advocating competency-based assessments and tests, while also arguing that these were better than traditional IQ and personality-based tests. His ideas have since been widely adopted in many organizations.

McClelland's second major contribution was in demonstrating, in India and elsewhere in the developing world, that it is possible to learn Achievement Motivation as an adult. Groups which do so, start more businesses that employ more people than comparison groups without achievement motivation training. A third major contribution is the field of competency modelling. McClelland wrote his seminal paper 'Testing for Competence Rather Than Intelligence' in 1973. His research indicated that although traditional academic aptitude tests and the test of knowledge (commonly used to choose from among applicants for jobs in the Foreign Service, civil service and elsewhere) were good predictors of academic performance, they seldom predicted outstanding on-the-job performance. He went on to argue that the best predictors of outstanding on-the-job performance were the underlying, enduring personal characteristics which he called 'competencies'. One example of a competency is the achievement motivation that characterizes outstanding entrepreneurs in India and elsewhere, and which was the foundation for McClelland's work—teaching achievement motivation to entrepreneurs and small business owners. Other competencies, such as Interpersonal Understanding, or Organizational Awareness, are more closely related to 'Emotional Intelligence'. Since then, McClelland's findings have been replicated, validated cross-culturally, and further developed by over 30 years of global competency research carried out by McBer and, later, by the HayGroup. Although different sets of competencies predict success in different roles, there are certain consistent patterns as well.

How We Study Competencies

The basic assumptions underlying competency research, as developed by McClelland, Boyatzis and others, are:

- Behavior is a function of the interaction between the person and the situation,

- Different behaviors, within a given type of situation, are likely to lead to different results, some more useful than others.

His assumptions produce a simple structure:

> Situation × Person → Behavior → Results

A very simple example is that of a student (person) in a course at school (situation), studying (behavior), and getting graded (result). If the student is curious (a characteristic of the person), the student will read widely and study broadly (behavior) and get excellent grades (result). 'Curiosity' would be one competency for such a student. Another student who is ambitious and diligent might see the course as useful for future advancement, study intensely and also get excellent grades. In this case, ambition and diligence would be competencies for the student.

> Situation × Person → Behavior → Results
> Course at school × Student → Studying → Grades
> Interesting course × Curious student → Extensive studying → Grades
> Useful course × Diligent, ambitious student → Intense studying → Grades

Competency research in the McClelland tradition, working backwards from the results to the person, discovers:

- o   the (relatively enduring) characteristics of the person
- o   which lead to outstanding results
- o   in a certain kind of situation (usually, a particular job or role).

In order to do this, we:

- Identify people who achieve outstanding results in a certain situation, e.g. being a CEO/CMD of a large company in India, at the turn of the millennium.

- Get those people to tell us very detailed stories about their work, in a three-hour Behavioral Event Interview, as described hereafter.
- Sort out the actual behaviors—what the person did, said, thought, and felt during these experiences, e.g. examples, quotes, and detailed descriptions of what the leader did and said.
- Group similar behaviors which express an underlying characteristic of a person e.g. 'Executive Maturity' or 'Adaptive Thinking'.[5]
- Count the people who displayed this behavior, that is, who possess this competency.

It is important to understand that the competencies described in this book are based on actual, work-related behaviors described by outstanding leaders in their Behavioral Event Interviews,[6] and not *on their theories or opinions about what is important,* nor *on anyone else's theories or opinions.*

For example, when a leader said, 'Empowering your people is important' or, 'I am good at empowering my people' or, even, 'That event was successful because I was able to empower my people', these statements were not counted as the basis for a competency.

On the other hand, when a CEO said:

I went to my team and I told them, 'Ignore other people's pressures, continue your work, keep on following your process and your own professional judgment, and I will accept your decision on this matter and protect you from interference' and then went on to provide details on how he followed through on this promise.

This statement did form a piece of evidence for the competency of 'Empowerment with Accountability'. Likewise, each competency in this model is built from the thousands of specific behaviors described by the outstanding Indian CEOs/ CMDs in their Behavioral Event Interviews.

The Structure of a Competency Model

A competency 'model' is an account of the set of personal characteristics and patterns of thought and behavior which lead to outstanding performance outcomes in a given job or role. An attempt is made to balance completeness with parsimony: this is partly a matter of consultant judgment and partly a matter of discriminant analysis. Generally, models for executive roles contain 5-13 competencies, grouped into 3-4 clusters.

Competency Clusters Allow for Many Different Versions of Excellence within the Same Model

Generally, we do not expect that even outstanding leaders will consistently demonstrate all of the competencies in the model because we recognize that there are many different paths to excellence. Instead, we group the competencies into clusters that represent alternate means to the same end, or alternate manifestations of the same underlying characteristic. Although to some extent, competencies within a cluster do tend to correlate with each other, this correlation is not the basis for the clustering. Rather, competencies are clustered according to the underlying orientation. In this model, these orientations are:

- Towards business issues for the first cluster of competencies (Socially Responsible Business Excellence);
- Towards the team for the second cluster (Energizing the Team);
- Towards the external factors for the third cluster (Managing the Environment); and

- Towards the underlying sources of the competencies (the leaders' Inner Strength, in the fourth cluster of the Indian CEO model).

In general, one would expect that outstanding leaders would demonstrate a 'balanced portfolio' of strengths in each of the clusters, but not necessarily in every competency. Indeed, that is what we observed in this research.

The Developmental Levels of Competencies

Each competency represents a characteristic of a leader. Each competency also contains a series of behaviors, all with the same general intent but with varying degrees of sophistication or completeness. These related behaviors form a developmental scale of four levels from the most basic manifestation of the competency to the behavior that is most sophisticated and most likely to add value to the organization.[7]

Each developmental level of the competencies was based on many examples of behaviors, drawn from the Behavioral Event Interviews. There were more instances of lower levels of competencies and fewer of higher levels. Some of the quotes used in creating the developmental scales are cited in the 'Pure for Sure' case study in Chapter 3, as well as in Chapters 8 through 11 where we discuss how the competencies interact in four critical types of business scenarios.

For the most part, these scales are based on the generic competency scales[8]—described in *Competence at Work*—shortened to include only those sections of the scale that are relevant to the Indian CEO. The developmental scales of the generic competencies, as well as the developmental scales of the unique competencies of the Indian CEO model, are shaped by developmental theory. They are also informed by our practical experience in writing and applying competency developmental scales. The theoretical underpinnings for each generic competency are noted in *Competence at Work*.

Summary of the Competency Research Methods

This study was conducted according to rigorous methods pioneered by McClelland, of the Harvard University, working in India and elsewhere, and was further developed at the McClelland Centre for Innovation and Research (HayGroup's research division based in Boston). These methods include the following:

Criterion Sampling

Leaders who are outstanding—according to a clear set of criteria—are studied and compared to a group that does not meet the criteria. Each Indian CEO, who was interviewed intensively, met all of the following criteria:

- Is the head of one of 100 financially best-performing companies in India;
- Is widely respected;
- Has sufficient tenure at the company to be a credible leader there; and
- Represents balanced sample across industries and sectors.

Behavioral Event Interviews (BEI)

The core of the competency method—the BEI—is a two-to-three hour, in-depth interview in which the participants provide detailed stories about their recent successes and failures, and what they did, said, thought, felt, and wanted to accomplish in dealing with these situations.

Expert Panels

Structured discussions with groups of industry experts and thought leaders provide the context and perspective to the challenges of the role and the necessary competencies. This study was conducted across six such panels covering CEOs, ex-CEOs, government officials, academicians and Indian MBA students at Harvard.

Coding

The BEI interviews are transcribed and the text is carefully compared and benchmarked against a list of 22 universal competencies in a structured coding process (see graphic sidebar for typical standards). In addition, other behaviors unique to the individual or the group are collected for qualitative analysis and possible inclusion in the final model.

(Box contd.)

(Box contd.)

Concept Formation

All the data is analyzed and synthesized in a five-day session to develop a competency model, which predicts outstanding performance on the job. Signe Spencer, co-author of *Competence at Work*, led the concept formation for the Indian CEO Competency model.

Performance Outcome Analysis

A recent innovation from the McClelland Centre, this process involves grouping the BEI stories according to the business challenges faced by the participants, and then sorting the stories by the effectiveness of the results achieved. This process helps identify which competencies lead to success in specific types of critical situations. In the Indian CEO study, four such situations were analyzed: Turnarounds, Building Capability, Launching New Operations, and Lobbying for Changes.

Validation

During validation, the findings from competency research are tested and fine-tuned, based on feedback from the new groups of participants. Validation panels for this study included relevant government ministers, business leaders, academicians and business students.

For the general reader, we shall now describe the competency model as it was developed for Indian CEOs: in an overview of the whole model at first, followed by an example of the kind of qualitative data used and how the competencies were coded (a case study pertaining to competencies) and then, through the details of each competency and how they were used in each of the four situations described most often by Indian CEOs.

Notes

1. D.C. McClelland, Allen Baldwin, Urie Bronfenbrenner, and Fred Strodbeck (1958), *Talent and Society: New Perspectives in the Identification of Talent*, Princeton, New Jersey, D. Van Nostrand. D.C. McClelland (1973). 'Testing for Competence Rather than Intelligence', *American Psychologist*, D.C McClelland (1998). 'Identifying competencies with behavioral event interviews', *Psychological Science*,

Vol. 9(5), pp. 331-39. For an overview and history of the method see Katherine Adams' interview with David McClelland (1997) published in *Competency*, Vol. 4(3), pp. 18-23. See also R.E. Boyatzis (1982), *The Competent Manager: A Model for Effective Performance*, John Wiley & Sons, New York. J.C. Flanagan (1954), 'The Critical Incident Technique', *Psychology Bulletin*, Vol. 51, pp. 327-58; W.W. Ronan and G.P. Latham (1974), 'The Reliability and Validity of the Critical Incident Technique: A Closer Look', *Studies in Personnel Psychology*, Vol. 6, 1974, pp. 53-64.

2. See significant advances in this area, particularly R.E. Boyatzis, *The Competent Manager: A Model for Effective Performance* (the first published empirical, cross-organizational study of competencies, based on Behavioral Event Interviews). R.E. Boyatzis (2006), 'Using tipping points of emotional intelligence and cognitive competencies to predict financial performance of leaders', *Psicothemia*, Vol. 17, 2006, pp. 124-31.

3. An entire consulting industry has grown up around the application of competencies, as well as a journal, *Competency*. See, for example, Paul A. Iles (1993), 'Achieving Strategic Coherence in HRD Through Competence-based Management and Organisation Development', *Personnel Review*, Vol. 22 (6), pp. 63-80. J. Hayes, A. Rose-Quirie, and C.W. Allinson (2000), 'Senior Manager's Perceptions of the Competencies they require for Effective Performance: Implications for Training and Development', *Personnel Review*, Vol. 29(1), pp. 92-105. In addition, there is a whole movement around teaching competence. See, for example, John Raven and John Stephenson (eds) (2001), *Competence in the Learning Society*, Peter Lang Publishing, UK.

4. A partial list of competency studies includes R.E. Boyatzis (1982), *The Competent Manager: A Model for Effective Performance*; J.P. Briscoe and D.T. Hall (1999), 'Grooming and Picking Leaders using Competency Frameworks: Do they Work?' *Organizational Dynamics*, Autumn, pp. 37-51; J.P. Campbell, M.D. Dunnette, E.E. Lawler III and K.E. Weick (1970), *Managerial Behavior, Performance, and Effectiveness*, McGraw Hill, New York; A.R.J. Dainty and M.I. Cheng (2005), 'Competency-based Model for Predicting Construction Project Managers' Performance', *Journal of Management in Engineering*, Vol. 21(1), pp. 2-9, H.D. Horch (2003), 'Competencies of Sport Managers in German Sport Clubs and Sport', *Managing Leisure*, Vol. 8(2), pp. 70-84; J.P. Kotter (1982), *The General Managers*, Free Press, New York; J.P. Kotter (1988), *The Leadership Factor*, Free Press, New York; J. Sandberg (2000), 'Understanding Human Competence

at Work: An Interpretative Approach', *Academy of Management Journal*, Vol. 43(1), pp. 9-25. For recent research with a similar methodology applied to entire enterprises see: Jim Collins (2001), *Good to Great: Why Some Companies Make the Leap...and Others Don't*, Harper Business, New York.

5. For the authoritative discussion of the process of grouping similar behaviours to 'code' text, see R.E. Boyatzis (1998), *Transforming Qualitative Information: Thematic Analysis and Code Development*, Sage Publications, Thousand Oaks, CA.

6. For a description of Behavioral Event Interview as practiced in this study see: Lyle M. Spencer and Signe Spencer (1993), *Competence at Work*, John Wiley & Sons, New York.

7. For more on the use of developmental scales with executives see D.C. McClelland (1998), 'Identifying Competencies with Behavioral Event Interviews', *Psychological Science*, Vol. 9(5), pp. 331-39. For description of tipping points in competencies with executives see R.E. Boyatzis (2006), 'Using tipping points of emotional intelligence and cognitive competencies to predict financial performance of leaders', *Psicothemia*, Vol. 17, pp. 124-31.

8. Lyle M. Spencer and Signe Spencer (1993), *Competence at Work*, John Wiley & Sons, New York.

3 | Introduction to the Indian CEO Model

An Overview of the Model of Excellence for Indian Business Leadership

The Indian CEO model comprises 11 competencies (i.e. endur-ing characteristics of the person which help him/her achieve outstanding results as a CEO in India) that can be arranged in four groups or 'Clusters' (Figure 3.1). Each cluster:

- contains 2–3 related competencies sharing a single pur-pose (i.e., they can be thought of as variations on a single theme);
- relates directly to a different aspect of the fundamen-tal role of an Indian CEO; and
- fits together and supports the other clusters in certain ways.

These aspects of the Indian CEO model are discussed here, as well as in Chapter 4, through the example of an interview, showing how the competencies fit together—in action—to produce an outstanding result. We shall discuss each cluster and its competencies in more detail in Chapters 5-9.

ON A PERSONAL NOTE...

We found a great deal to admire in these interviews, even though some of us (Signe Spencer, Tharuma Rajah) have extensive experience in assessing executives and CEOs, and in building leadership models around the world, and are not often impressed. The personal character, the concern for the social impact of their business decisions and the general inner strength demonstrated by the CEOs who participated in the interviews were most impressive, as were their cooperation and generosity in discussing their experiences.

Figure 3.1: The Indian CEO Competency Model

Socially Responsible Business Excellence
- Adaptive Thinking
- Entrepreneurial Drive
- Excellence in Execution

Energizing the Team
- Driving Change
- Team Leadership
- Empowerment with Accountability

Managing Environment
- Networking
- Organizational Awareness
- Stakeholder Influence

Inner Strength
- Executive Maturity
- Transcending Self

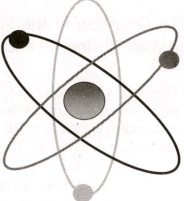

Four Clusters of Competencies, in the Context of Enterprise Leadership in India

One of the most striking aspects of the stories told by Indian leaders is their single-minded focus on growth—not just of their own business but of the Indian economy on the whole. They demonstrated amazing energy, determination and persistence against extraordinary challenges posed by the problems pertaining to supply chain and infrastructure, permissions from the government, external criticism and difficult union relations. Indian leaders, in spite of these difficulties, focused their impressive intellects on transforming their businesses so as to better serve their country and help accelerate its economic growth. Their concern for their impact on the development of India appeared to be the reason behind many a business risk—be it their determination to make a turnaround successful ('India needs this facility') or to introduce a new product ('The farmers in this region need a tractor better-designed for their conditions' or, 'The growing middle class needs the ability to finance home-ownership, and not to always rent their homes').

Compared to their counterparts in other countries, Indian leaders showed an unusually consistent and pervasive concern for the good of their country, along with a related focus on providing goods and services which benefit everyone (utilities, infrastructure), on addressing the practical needs of the lower-half of the economic pyramid (salt, soap, tractors, paper, fertilizer, financial facilities, reliable consumer goods) or, for that matter, on enhancing India's pride and stature when it comes to its technical capabilities (certain high-tech projects) vis-à-vis the global community.

The central and most important responsibility of the Indian CMD or CEO is to create a sound and sustainable business model that delivers meaningful value to all internal and external shareholders in a manner which ensures that the benefits are spread across the spectrum of Indian society. This fundamental task—core of the Indian CEO model—is directly addressed by the three competencies in the competency cluster that we call the **SCRIBE Cluster of Competencies.**

- **Socially Responsible Business Excellence (SCRIBE) Cluster of Competencies:** This is the ability to make 'hard' decisions about strategy and its execution and the allocation of resources (when and in what to invest), while keeping firmly in mind the parameters of societal welfare.

The **SCRIBE** competencies form the purpose and the core of this leadership model. They are supported by and enacted through three other, *equally important* clusters of competencies, each one reflecting a crucial aspect of the role of the Indian CEO model:

- **'Energizing the Team' Cluster of Competencies:** Success does not rest on an excellent business model alone; the leader must also focus personal attention on the needs of the organization—and the people in the organization—inspiring their best efforts, bringing out the best in them both as individuals and as a team so that they are empowered to implement the business model or the vision.

- **'Managing the Environment' Cluster of Competencies:** Simultaneously, the leader must facilitate the organization's relationship with the external world. Often, this means personal involvement with, and personal influence on, various constituencies outside the organization itself.

- **'Inner Strength' Cluster of Competencies:** During this demanding and challenging activity, the leader is sustained by his/her own inner strength. It is this personal inner strength that makes the leadership—and the leader's influence on others within and outside the organization—both credible and effective. Without his/her inner strength, the leader may be unable to sustain the efforts and the credibility necessary to be successful.

The leader's attention to the needs of the organization—which enables the organization to execute his/her direction and vision—is manifested in the competencies of **Energizing the Team:** the ability to keep the energy levels of his/her teams pumped up, in order to ensure complete involvement on a sustainable and ongoing basis, and to show faith in the team by delegation of authority and accountability.

Leaders must also manage their relations with the external environment, often serving as the interface between their organization and the larger world. Especially important and difficult, this role is seen in the competencies of **Managing the Environment:** the leader's ability to sustain positive and synergistic relationships with external organizations including the competitors, the unions, the media, academic institutions and, most significantly, the government.

And, because all this is so difficult, the leaders need to sustain, and be sustained by, their personal sources of direction, determination, and stamina—his/her *Inner Strength*: the inherent personal qualities of impeccable character, a sense of fair-play and justice, a high level of emotional and mental stability, and an ability to think beyond the 'me', make a leader a true leader who also serves as a role model for his/her employees to follow.

Table 3.1: Brief Definitions of the Competencies of the Indian CEO Model

Competency Name	Brief Definition of the Competency
'Socially Responsible Business Excellence Cluster'	
• Adaptive Thinking	Strategic insight into business, adapting methods and technology to the Indian situation and to address unmet needs (with a special focus on the bottom of the pyramid)
• Entrepreneurial Drive	Unleashing the spirit of entrepreneurship and competitiveness to find new horizons of growth
• Excellence in Action	Foresight plus fierce and unrelenting passion to execute/act today, to improve the future
'Energizing the Team' Cluster	
• Team Leadership	Inspiring and protecting the team, enabling excellent team performance

(Table 3.1 contd.)

(*Table 3.1 contd.*)

Competency Name	Brief Definition of the Competency
• *Driving Change*	Leading the organization to implement and embed sustainable change
• *Empowerment with Accountability*	Delegating authority to allow others to act with purpose and accountability
'Managing the Environment' Cluster	
• *Networking*	Reaching out to an extensive network for ideas and problem-solving
• *Organizational Awareness*	Understanding how things get decided and done in a particular organization
• *Stakeholder Influence*	Using customized strategies to influence specific stakeholders
'Inner Strength' Cluster	
• *Transcending Self*	Courageous dedication to the super-ordinate goals: doing what is right and what will make India great
• *Executive Maturity*	Emotional wisdom to respond to others and embody the aspirations of the organization

Thus, **SCRIBE** makes for the core of the leader's excellence—with a balance between internal attention in *Energizing the Team* and external attention in **Managing the Environment.** The whole model is supported and sustained by the leader's **Inner Strength.** The competencies within each cluster have related purposes and draw on similar or related skills. Although, to some extent, these competencies support or reinforce each other, they also can be seen as alternate means to the same or a similar end. To that extent, they can substitute for each other.

Indian leaders need to take into consideration all four key aspects of leadership, each one addressed by a cluster of two or three different competencies (Table 3.1). These competencies are drawn from the real-life experiences as described by outstanding Indian CEOs in long, detailed, Behavioral Event Interviews conducted by senior consultants. Although we have provided a structure to organize the innumerable thoughts, feelings, actions and speeches described to us (through our interviews with the Indian CEOs), the content for these competencies comes from the business leaders themselves, from their actual experiences in leading their businesses. The following chapter offers a sample of the data on which this model is based.

4 A Case Study of Competencies in Action

Before we discuss each competency in detail, in the four chapters that follow, let us first see how these competencies appear in action. The 'PURE for SURE' case study represents one story taken from one of the interviews. This story, besides being interesting, provides a sample of the material from which the competencies were developed, so that the reader can understand the basis for our findings. Each interviewee provided two to four such stories. The story also demonstrates one way in which the competencies fit together to produce excellent results for the business as well as for India.

A Case Study based on a Behavioral Event Interview
with the Chief Executive

'PURE for SURE'

(This case study shows the developmental levels of *Driving Change*, and how other competencies are integrated to support this change.)

Text from the interview (edited only slightly for conciseness)	*Notes on the competencies* (as seen in the text)
The most important thing was the realization that customer wants pure, unadulterated product, either diesel or petrol. That came from the visioning exercise. The staff wanted	*Adaptive Thinking*: altering the business to serve the needs of the consumer and of the country.

to achieve customer satisfaction. We did a lot of market surveys and they all showed that it is the key issue in the mind of the customer. We engaged a strategy consulting firm who also came up with the same idea and worked on the various steps we would have to take to ensure that happens.

This includes a form of *Networking*, using market surveys, to understand the customer.

Although one could see that providing pure products would benefit India at large, *transcending self* was not counted here because the leader was not explicit about this aspect of the situation.

The crux of the issue was, how do we face the dealer who is making a lot of money today selling adulterated products when by selling Pure or Sure, he will lose money.

Organizational Awareness: understanding the perspectives and situation of the dealer and how that impacted the organization.

Some of the staff had been beaten over this so they were not willing to come forward. In meetings they would agree, but in reality, nothing would happen. So unless we attacked that single issue, the whole scheme would not work.

Organizational Awareness about the reactions of the staff and how the violence impacted their behavior. *Driving Change, Level 1:* planning and identifying the most important obstacle.

We had a series of informal meetings at various places. I was encouraging the middle managers to go ahead. So in all meetings, I used to continuously emphasize that we had to introduce this initiative.

Driving Change, Level 2: constant communication of the change.

Whenever I heard that some staff has done something in this area, then immediately I would stop and find out what they did, why they did it. Then, I told them 'I am here. If there is any problem, give me a ring.'...

A hint of *Empowerment with Accountability* though without enough details to count it here.

Even though sometimes I felt a little low, I was confident that this can take place, provided the staff is fully motivated on this aspect and if the staff knows that this vital for the success of the company as a whole, then they will come forward and do it.

Executive Maturity: recognizing and managing his own feelings, understanding and trusting the staff.

So the Business Unit (BU) Head said, 'I am prepared to do that. If you give me support, I am prepared to take it further.' I was feeling glad. At last somebody is coming forward to do it. But, how do we convince the staff that they should do it? Then we said, 'When you go to a distributor for testing and sealing, etc., then have the protection of the police, or if the police are not coming forward then make it known to the public so that people in that area are aware that one of the companies is doing something and that various people are against it.' It was my idea. I told the BU Head we should try this, because we wanted to break that psychology. We wanted to ensure that the staff learn that actually this could happen. The next step was to introduce this concept at one outlet. So, the BU Head went to an outlet where it was mandated to his staff to introduce this concept and also to tell the public that that outlet was providing this unadulterated product. Once this was done, sales picked up tremendously. Then the BU Head immediately said, 'Okay, fine, now the next step of the process is to call the dealers and see why is this happening, and draw volunteers for this process.' I thought they are breaking the ice somewhere but still, the majority of the dealers are opposing.

Driving Change, Level 2: continuing to communicate the desired change and to provide support for it.

Excellence in Execution: persistence in trying different tactics to ensure that this change happens.

There was an incident where the staff was beaten and the police harassed him. I told him that the company would do everything in its capacity to protect him, but the final decision would be with the individual. The officer said that if the company was with him, he was willing to take the risks. Basically I wanted to give them the support, tell him that I was there for him, and he should go ahead. That was the only message.

Empowerment with Accountability: providing support to the staff, and supporting the staff's decision without determining what the decision would be 'the final decision would be with the individual'.

The BU Head rang me and told me that the staff had been attacked. I thought now here is an occasion that we had to prove that the entire company is with him and therefore

More *Empowerment with Accountability* by supporting the staff.

the dealers cannot take us for a ride. We had to prove this point. We had to put that behind him, behind his staff. So then I told him to contact the Ministry and go to the police, and also told them to publish an article in the press that that is what has happened.

Excellence in Execution (urgency of action, and determination, persistence against obstacles).

The beginning of *Level 4* of *Driving Change*, involving the public media to support and ensure the sustainability of the change.

He was really very intelligent so I was only suggesting the various things he could do. After some time, the dealers' efforts failed and we could take the samples and at a later date of course the outlet was terminated. That was really the turning point when the dealers realized that one of the companies was intent on doing this and not only at one outlet, that tomorrow it could happen in other places. They began to understand that we meant business, we wanted to provide better service to the customer, and we would do everything possible for that.

Stakeholder Influence: influencing the Dealers Community by using a Dramatic/ Symbolic Action of running an outlet with his own staff, and providing pure products there.

When a new outlet was commissioned very close to one of our stations, I said, 'Why can't this outlet be run by our staff?' Basically, to tell the dealers that this outlet can provide better service to the customer in terms of the quality and quantity, and other services. I wanted to give this message to the dealers' community. The sales at that outlet increased but then the five other outlets in that area, no customers would go there. The dealers were up in arms, they put all sort of problems to the staff there. They used to send the Weights and Measures department in the "government" to check each dispenser, which meant that we had to stop traffic and the inspector would check all the items as per the rule book and point out small things that may not have been done. Another method of giving a problem was when the

Driving Change, Level 3: starting to institutionalize the change by setting up a different structure of running the outlets.

staff were returning home. There would be a car coming from the opposite side that would come very close, but not actually hit them.

I was only thinking that we should succeed. The staff should not succumb to it. I went to that outlet, and said to the staff, 'If you feel that you are strong enough to take on these things, nothing will happen, nobody will do anything further.' I wanted to give them the encouragement that we are supporting them... 'So don't go back on this and this is very, very vital for the company. You have to provide better customer service. That is the vision we have chosen', and this is what they have to do for the fulfilment of that vision. So they agreed, and in spite of all the problems it was going on. After maybe 2 or 3 months, the dealers realized that we were serious so their efforts came down. And other dealers volunteered to participate in this process.

I feel we have done something. Then I was telling this story everywhere to give them an example of what has happened at one outlet, so why not do the same at some of the outlets in their territories. I wanted it to be replicated throughout the country. It is not enough that we have one achievement. I want this to happen throughout the country. If that does not happen it will not have any meaningful effect. So I want volunteers to come forward. I do not want to push it through because enough pushing has been done earlier. I now wanted volunteers to come forward to take on this assignment and then do it on their own. It started slowly, but now there are almost a thousand **Such outlets.**

Excellence in Execution: perseverance and determination in executing a very difficult change; 'I was only thinking that we should succeed' and then acting on that thought.

Executive Maturity: providing a personal example of determination to provide pure products, inspiring the courage of the staff.

Driving Change by continually communicating and supporting the change.

Driving Change, Levels 2 and 3: continuing to communicate the desired change and to build it into the normal practices of the company. Notice how he is shifting the drive and responsibility for this change toward the employees who are now volunteering.

Entrepreneurial Drive in setting a specific, measurable goal (to replicate this change throughout the country). Additional *Entrepreneurial Drive* by increasing market or profit is implied but is not explicit in this story and so was not counted here.

Basically people want to do things, but they face a lot of hindrances. It is the duty of whoever is in a position of authority to recognize those hindrances and then give them support. Only then the do the staff feel committed and be part of the change process.

Here the leader provides a clear statement about *Executive Maturity* and *Empowerment with Accountability* that were demonstrated earlier in the case study. However, this statement alone would not be counted for the competencies.

It has sent a very strong message to not only the dealers but also to the oil companies that they cannot adulterate. The people, the media, and the Supreme Court have also sent the same message. One gentleman said that if our company can assure the customers of pure, high quality products, why you others cannot do it too? I felt very glad, very glad that we had reached the highest level of quality.

Driving Change: level 4, involving external institutions- the media and even the courts to cement the change.

This case study shows how competencies are combined to achieve a business result, improving the performance of the organization. Note that though competencies from all four clusters are combined in this story, the bulk of the emphasis is on **Energizing the Team** (*Driving Change*, and *Empowerment with Accountability*), which is appropriate for this situation in particular. In other types of situations different competencies come onto the forefront, as will be seen in the chapters on 'Scenario Analysis'. As you may have also noticed, some competencies are implicit or suggested in the case study (*Transcending Self* and higher levels of *Entrepreneurial Drive*) but were not described in sufficient detail to be 'counted' in this part of this interview. This provides an example of the degree of rigor in 'coding' or counting competencies.

In the chapters that follow, we shall take a more detailed look at the competencies in each cluster. Remember, each competency in the Indian CEO model, and in the international benchmarks, is based on dozens or even hundreds of examples like the ones in this chapter.

I

Cluster of Competencies

5 Socially Responsible Business Excellence

The **Socially Responsible Business Excellence (SCRIBE)** cluster covers much of what people may ordinarily think of as business acumen, business sense or, more simply, the knack of doing business. The trio of competencies comprising this cluster is the founding stone to the role of a chief executive officer (CEO), as well as to the financial health of the business over the years. These competencies within the SCRIBE cluster enable the leader to make sound business decisions, shape future vision, determine the company's risk-taking abilities and define the company's capabilities to absorb and experiment with new business practices and newer emerging technologies.

The CEOs involved in our study are the crème de la crème of India, Inc., each having used the business-focused competencies in a very socially responsible manner.

The three competencies in the **Socially Responsible Business Excellence** cluster are:

1. *Adaptive Thinking*: Strategic insight into the business, adapting innovative methods and technology to the Indian situation and to address unmet market needs (with a special focus on the bottom half of the economic pyramid).
2. *Entrepreneurial Drive*: Unleashing the spirit of entrepreneurial competitiveness to find new horizons of growth.
3. *Excellence in Execution*: Foresight combined with fierce and unrelenting passion to execute/act today, to improve the future.

The first competency, *Adaptive Thinking*, provides a leader with openness and an ability to think beyond the current state of the business. Here, the leader does not believe that the company has the best ideas and is willing to find, adapt and utilize the best-of-the-breed practices, innovations and technologies from across the globe. However, the leader does not stop at finding the best practices from elsewhere, but goes on to adapt them, making changes suitable to Indian conditions. The second competency, *Entrepreneurial Drive*, drives the leader to find newer vistas for growth and take the firm to uncharted areas, experiment with newer business models; even, when necessary, break conventions and set new standards where none existed before. The third competency, *Excellence in Execution*, bridges the gap between the blueprints and the results—the budgets and the outcomes—and provides the sense of urgency and focus which ensures that goals are accomplished within a reasonable (or even a very challenging) time-frame.

When Socially Responsible Business Excellence is Most Applicable

The SCRIBE competencies are most effective in turnaround and start-up situations, and have many obvious applications in both these situations. In all of the most effectively crafted turnarounds, leaders used the highest level of *Adaptive Thinking*—developing a new, strategic insight or a new business model to ensure the longer-term success of their enterprises. In the less successful turnaround stories, leaders invariably use lower levels of *Adaptive Thinking*, that is, they do not find and implement a new strategy or experiment with a new business model. As one might expect, the *Excellence in Execution* competency also comes into play both in turnaround and in start-up situations.

Another revelation of the study was that most Indian CEOs also use *Adaptive Thinking* while building their organization's capabilities. However, an important caveat, if the leader who is trying to build capability in the organization is far *too* involved in his own *Excellence in Execution* or his personal *Entrepreneurial Drive*, then he risks alienating both his team and his workforce. He may not involve and stimulate other people's personal investment in increasing organizational capacity. A team effort is imperative in such situations. So, in this particular situation, some of the SCRIBE competencies (especially *Adaptive Thinking*) are helpful but the balance of the leader's thoughts and efforts should be focused on *Energizing the Team*—thereby stimulating *the* **Socially Responsible Business Excellence** *of the team*, not only his/her personal agenda. This was shown in the 'Pure for Sure' case study (Chapter 4) where the leader used the **Energizing the Team** competencies of *Driving Change* and *Empowerment with Accountability* more often—and with more attention than he did the SCRIBE competencies—even though these were also present and important to the success of the event. It is this *balance* between the SCRIBE competencies and the others that is crucial.

A note of caution: when lobbying the government, the business-oriented approach was actually counter-productive. Most of the frustrating examples of lobbying the government included *Adaptive Thinking*, while, in the more effective examples of lobbying with the government, the leaders seemed to set aside their business thinking for that moment, focusing instead on the other two sets of competencies: **Inner Strength** and **Managing the Environment.** When lobbying with the government or otherwise engaged in boundary management, the patience and persistence that characterize **Inner Strength** was found to be more useful than the sense of urgency that characterises *Excellence in Execution.*

Adaptive Thinking

> CEOs need to be adaptable in today's context.
> This is a skill set required in the modern context.
>
> ~ **Kumar Mangalam Birla**
> Chairman, Aditya Birla Group
>
> Adaptive thinking is very necessary
> given the stage of development in which we are.
>
> ~ **D.S. Brar**
> Former CEO/MD, Ranbaxy Laboratories Ltd.

Today, given the unique juncture at which India Inc. finds itself, the need to devise strategies that are effective and give a competitive edge over a sustained period is one of the main challenges that an Indian leader faces, day in and day out. It is one front where, interestingly, Indian CEOs—contrary to popular perception—do well. While Indian leaders (in our study) show a unique eagerness and capability in adapting the best in class innovations, practices and technologies, the real beauty lay in their excellent customization—that 'Indian' touch—be it the latest HR tools, or quality initiatives like Six Sigma, or rolling out software packages like SAP. It was striking how technologies or business practices were generally not adopted 'as is' from other countries, but were modified and adapted to suit the Indian situation. In a few cases, even new technologies or new business models were created especially to address local conditions.

While, at times, Indian CEOs were personally innovative, their special skill seems to lie in finding and adapting other people's (sometimes from other countries') innovations to suit their own situation and needs. Often *Adaptive Thinking* was paired with *Networking*—where leaders established and used a wide range of contacts to find the information and innovations they needed to adapt. Prime examples of leaders who effectively embody this competency would be from the software industry—such as Nandan Nilekani, S. Ramadorai, and Ramalinga Raju. However, this kind of thinking was found across the sectors, not only in the 'high tech' industries: CEOs found new markets for their fertilizers, and set up newer—and fairer—distribution channels for farmers; built a new business model for paper production (one that empowered Indian farmers and is more sustainable); adapted tractor designs to suit the needs and lands of the Indian farmers; and adapted Western technologies that were originally meant for another purpose so as to effectively use the less expensive grades of fuel that were readily available in India—without compromising the quality of the output.

Another unique revelation was the special focus and attention that the middle-class and the lower strata of society received from these CEOs: many had geared their companies to cater to this huge segment of the Indian society. The bottom of the pyramid was on the crosshair of many CEOs; each one proactively taking actions to engage and develop a relationship with that segment. Though each had different methods, some were providing reliable, good quality products at cheap prices, while some others were providing services like options for cheaper finance. Yet others were launching innovative channels like *e-Choupal*, the rural initiative and *Project Shakti*, the distribution scheme respectively launched by ITC and HLL.

Box 5.1: Developmental Levels of *Adaptive Thinking*

Strategic insight into business, adapting innovative methods and technology to the Indian situation and to address unmet market needs (especially at the bottom half of the economic pyramid)

Business insight based on understanding:

1. *The business model*
   - How this business makes money or delivers value
2. *The Indian market and business environment*
   - Meets unexpressed or unmet needs, often at the bottom half of the economic pyramid
3. *Innovative or adapted ideas*
   - Adapts technology and best practices to suit Indian scenarios
   - Finds and supports new solutions
4. *A new strategic direction*
   - Redefines the business direction- to respond effectively to the changing environment and opportunities

---

Entrepreneurial Drive

...the task of a successful CEO in a fully competitive market is to [motivate his internal team and] successfully meet external competitive pressure through innovation and efficiency.

~ Dr Manmohan Singh
Prime Minister of India

Entrepreneurial Drive is the relentless quest for efficiency, excellence and global standards—a dream that propels the leader to make a mark on the global stage, a pursuit that drives leaders to flirt with the idea of making the term 'worldclass' a part of their organizational DNA. It fuels the desire to create a place in the global pecking order, to seek a place not in the *Economic Times* 500 but to find its name in the *Fortune* 500 list. *Entrepreneurial Drive* is a fire that is stoked by a deep sense of ambition (for oneself, or for one's company or, for that matter, even for India). This ambition is a cocktail of innovation—be it a new business model or a disruptive technology or a unique marketing technique—and sound business sense.

It is important that, while the entrepreneurial fires stoke, the actions do not cross over to the realm of economic nonsense, something witnessed during the dotcom boom. Economic and financial sanity should prevail and things like return on capital, cost benefit analysis and profitability ratios, among others, cannot be ignored. No doubt, risks are inevitable in the fast changing business scenario but outstanding leaders are making non-stop efforts to mitigate that risk through their knowledge of the market, their sound business and economic analysis and their efficient implementation.

It is becoming ever more important to accurately understand the true cost of capital now, especially in the public sector where this cost may be obscured by the government's role in investment. (The issue of obscuring the true costs of business is not limited to India. It has also been famously problematic in certain private sector corporations in the US—ranging from corporations like Enron to Delphi—and evoking greater reporting and oversight requirements in the form of Sarbanes-Oxley regulations.)

Box 5.2: Developmental Levels of *Entrepreneurial Drive*

The spirit of entrepreneurship and competitiveness
to find new horizons of bottom-line growth

Growth and improvement based on:

1. *Pursuit of Excellence*
   - Finds better, faster, more efficient ways
2. *Competition and Global Standards*
   - Sets challenging, world-class goals to improve performance
3. *Detailed economic shape for the future*
   - Uses advanced financial models to shape direction
   - Pursues a detailed vision of the future, with energy and persistence
4. *New horizons of growth*
   - Takes entrepreneurial risks to enable the business to grow in new areas

---

Excellence in Execution

> Clearly defined progress is essential. People like to talk and talk and talk and have a lot of philosophical discussions. You need that but you also need to understand that you will devote only so long to discussion. After that you must come to very clearly defined targets, leading people into delivering execution.
>
> ~ **Ravi Kant**
> Executive Director–Commercial Vehicle Business Unit, Tata Motors

It is simple. CEOs walk the talk—and do not 'talk and talk and talk' as cited here by Ravi Kant. Like any leader will say, execution is the key to the success of any enterprise, and the fact also remains that excellence in execution has to be demonstrated by the top man in order to have a trickle down effect in the organization. History has shown that only those business leaders who act succeed. Often, a proactive problem-solving approach is a key to their success. It is only people with a sense of urgency and a clear focus on deliverables who create and manage industries and business empires. A common quality that runs through these leaders is a fiercely passionate determination on behalf of their organization, and the ability to keep fighting till success is achieved—even if odds are stacked heavily against them. They respond flexibly to their environment and ensure that action taken is appropriate to the context and to what is required.

Excellence in Execution embodies the urgency and the passion for action that is required in order to translate the good ideas of *Adaptive Thinking* and/or *Entrepreneurial Drive* into actual changes in the organization. Sometimes it is demonstrated by thinking ahead and taking action today (gathering information, starting the process of gaining the necessary permits, exploring potential new directions with one's peers in other organizations, putting contingency plans in place so that people in the organization know how to respond if things don't go as well as hoped). More often, *Excellence in*

Execution is demonstrated in the determination and persistence that is required to make the needed changes.

In large organizations, leaders also need to use the competencies of the **Energizing the Team** cluster to communicate their own focus on action to the rest of the organization so that all concerned have a buy-in in the actions and its rewards. But, again, this is top driven, and this process generally starts with the leader's foresight in *Excellence in Execution*.

Box 5.3: Developmental Levels of *Excellence in Execution*

Foresight and fierce, unrelenting passion to execute or act today, to improve the future

Focuses energy and persistence to address:

1. *Current problems*
   - Takes quick decisions and actions to address problems
2. *Upcoming problems*
   - Plans ahead to prevent crises
3. *Current opportunities*
   - Recognizes and acts on upcoming opportunities
   - Takes actions now to create short-term business potential
4. *Long-term potentials*
   - Focuses on re-defining the business for global positioning
   - Takes action now to create opportunities for future success

---

Socially Responsible Business Excellence: Compared to their Counterparts Worldwide, Indian Leaders Excel in Some Areas, Lag in Others

No doubt, Indian leaders are an intelligent lot. They display intellectual flexibility in getting to the heart of business issues and, then, finding ways to adapt ideas so as to make them work here (in India) successfully. These outstanding

Indian leaders (in the HayGroup study) displayed a concentrated focus on entrepreneurial growth, with most of their stories centred on this issue in one form or another. Compared to their counterparts worldwide, this group of Indian CEOs equal or surpass their outstanding counterparts around the world on *Entrepreneurial Drive* and on the strategic and innovative aspects of **Socially Responsible Business Excellence** (especially *Adaptive Thinking*).

Figure 5.1 compares the percentage of outstanding Indian CEOs demonstrating Level 3 or Level 4 of the SCRIBE competencies, with the percentages of groups of 30 truly outstanding and 16 more typical CEOs from the HayGroup database.

However, Indian CEOs were somewhat less likely to show foresight in executing changes (the *Excellence in Execution* competency). This finding is partly consistent with the comments of many of the experts in our discussion panels,

Figure 5.1: CEOs with 'Business Excellence' Competencies (Level 3 or Higher)

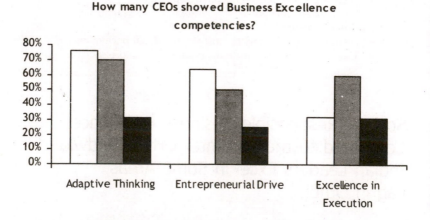

How many CEOs showed Business Excellence competencies?

Business Excellence competencies at level 3 or higher, or generic equivalent demonstrated in the interviews

☐ Best Indian ▨ Best International ■ Typical International

who recognized India's strengths in thinking through complex problems but also expressed concern about relative lack of execution of those good ideas. However, our findings (that the Indian leaders show only somewhat less *Excellence in Execution*) suggest that many of the difficulties in execution in India may have less to do with the leader's own focus on execution than with problems in managing the political and bureaucratic environment, dealing with structural and infra-structure related difficulties or, possibly, in motivating and managing the workforce.

6 Energizing the Team

CEOs should make it visible to others (walk the talk) that meritocracy is given due respect...only then would people see the relevance of HR systems such as Appraisal, Training, etc.

~ **Kumar Mangalam Birla**
Chairman, Aditya Birla Group

Every leader would have to do as Lord Krishna did at the beginning of the war between the Pandavas and the Kauravas,[1] motivating, cajoling, directing and invoking enthusiasm into his team, much like Krishna did with Arjuna. Teams can be powerful and effective only if the team leader is able to harness and, then, channel the team's energies so as to make the strategies bear fruit and help the organization achieve the best results. The leader must engage the energy and thoughts of all employees to work in tandem to achieve the organization's common goals. The journey is much more enjoyable this way. Often, many leaders are mistaken in their belief that their jobs are all about directing the ongoing activities of their teams. The difference between a good leader and a great one is that the latter realizes that the leader must not only direct the current activities of the team, but also build up their capabilities for the future, while engaging and strengthening their competencies. Outstanding Indian leaders use the competencies of **Energizing the Team** to ensure that their changes are well executed, *and* that their organization is strengthened with a view to the future.

The three competencies in the **Energizing the Team** cluster are:

- *Team Leadership*: The ability to take on a leadership role of inspiring and protecting the team, enabling excellent team performance.
- *Driving Change*: The ability to personally lead the organization to implement and embed sustainable change.
- *Empowerment with Accountability*: The maturity to delegate authority, enabling others to act with purpose and accountability.

The leader's role is particularly crucial during times of transformation within the organization, when it comes to directing the change and ensuring its long-term sustainability. Although there are many possible ways in which leaders can drive and sustain change in their organization, the Indian leaders we studied used an unusually consistent—and logical—pattern of leadership throughout the change process. This pattern is reflected in the competency of *Driving Change*.

Moreover, different sets of situations test different competencies. For example, leaders must also nurture and grow their teams, supporting their team's success during times of comparatively 'steady state', when no alarm bells are ringing. This task calls for somewhat different behaviors, like the *Team Leadership* competency, which are more supportive of the team's functioning and tend more toward building up the capability of the team, rather than making and sustaining a particular change.

Finally, leaders must simultaneously empower their people and hold them accountable, thus fostering their development and their ability to take on greater responsibilities (*Empower-ment with Accountability*). The days of autocratic leaders and micro-managers have long gone.

This cluster is particularly important, as the leader's ef-forts to develop people are distributed throughout the com-petencies in this cluster. Specific learning and development are usually included in a change process, in communicating and institutionalizing the change (*Driving Change*). A leader's role in *Team Leadership* ensures that general learning and development take place. On occasions the leader may per-sonally mentor and develop certain individuals, but in most cases the leader ensures that the appropriate learning and development takes place either through direct training or shar-ing experiences and delegating responsibility (*Empowerment with Accountability*).

When Energizing the Team is Most Relevant

In scenarios of start-ups or in building up the organization, the entire **Energizing the Team** cluster adds significant value. Again, in scenarios of organizational turnarounds, *Driving Change* and *Empowerment with Accountability* are basic, but vital, requirements in the repertoire of a CEO's skills. In all three situations, the leader adds value primarily by *facilitat-ing other people's performance*—which makes for the core of all the **Energizing the Team** competencies. In the Indian busi-ness environment, most leaders did not use these competen-cies very often while lobbying with the government or managing boundaries. Instead, they tended to shelter their teams from distractions coming from outside the organiza-tion. The one competency of **Energizing the Team** that did appear in stories about managing relationships with the gov-ernment and other external bodies was *Empowerment with Accountability*. This competency appeared when outside forces were attempting to influence certain decisions being made by the organization. In these cases, the leader sometimes gave the authority to make a decision (to chose a supplier, to design a product, etc.) to certain teams of experts, and then protected their decisions from external influence.

Team Leadership

> The CEO has to be an institution builder and a team builder... Communicating with people—having good people skills, reaching out by physically meeting them, supporting them with messages on important occasions, motivating them—is a must for a CEO to be successful.
>
> ~ **Rajendra Singh**
> Ex-CMD, NTPC, and Chairman,
> Mumbai Integrated Special Economic Zone Ltd.

Outstanding leaders take actions with a view to make the team more effective as a whole, ensuring it (either the executive team or the organization as a whole) has the support and guidance to deliver desired outcomes. These actions of the leader provide the foundation for a well-functioning team: a clear sense of direction and purpose; an understanding of how all the parts of the organization fit together to achieve their goals; the necessary training and education to perform their roles; clear and enforced rules about how the teams behave with each other; resources and freedom from distraction needed to do the job. Their roles are similar to those of a conductor of, say, the Philharmonic Orchestra; ensuring that each one knows his/her role and that the coordinated effort leads to the success of the team as a whole. *They measure their success through the success of others.* In many ways, *Team Leadership* used by Indian CEOs resembled the Level 5 leadership described by Jim Collins in his book *Good to Great*.[2] More focused on their teams and their organizations than on personal glory, these leaders worked quietly, behind the scenes, to ensure that their organizations achieved the best. At the heart of this competency is the self-image of a leader who takes responsibility to ensure that the team, the organization, performs at its very best.

Team Leadership generally appears as a long series of coordinated and consistent actions to strengthen and support the team in running the enterprise—rather than as a single action. *Team Leadership* sometimes supports *Driving Change*, but most often comes into play at times when the organization is not in the process of significant transformation or turbulent times and the ships are sailing in relatively calm waters.

Box 6.1: Developmental Levels of *Team Leadership*

The ability to take on a leadership role, inspiring and protecting the team, enabling excellent team performance.

Demonstrates Leadership by:

1. *Communicating effectively*
   - Shares information, rationale, checks for understanding
2. *Promoting team effectiveness*
   - Creates the internal conditions that allow the team to perform at its best, (for example, providing development norms and procedures during meetings, clarity of purpose and direction, or whatever conditions the team needs)
3. *Protecting the team and obtaining resources*
   - Provides needed resources, information, protection from distraction and 'manages the boundary' with the external world for the team
4. *Inspiring confidence and increasing morale*
   - Takes action to engage people to address business challenges and to deliver high standards of performance.
   - Takes actions to inspire confidence in the organization's strategy and its ability to deliver.

Driving Change

It is the role of the CEO to minimize the role of uncertainty within the organization by providing continuity, vision of the future and a clear plan to accomplish it.

~ **S. Varadarajan**
President, Indian National Science Academy

It is not enough for leaders to think of a new business model, or a needed change in the direction of the organization. They must also execute these changes, bringing the whole organization in line with their vision. The characteristic Indian style of leading change is to think through the change in a systematic manner, including all the necessary adjustments to the system and structure of the organization. This is the heart of *Driving Change*.

Outstanding CEOs make their organizations future-proof, by adapting to the changing needs of the business, by engaging their employees in the change process and institutionalizing this change as an integral part of the organization. The best Indian leaders chronologically follow a four-step process of change management: First, they plan the change and, most importantly, how it will be communicated and implemented. Second, they repeatedly articulate the desired changes *and the reasons for change and why it is important*, on many different platforms, and at many different levels within their organizations. This is a time-consuming but essential process. Third, they make changes in the organization's structure, processes and procedures to ensure the continued success of the change initiative by adopting and structuring it into the organization's culture. Four, the leader, in some cases, makes the commitment to change known publicly through newspapers or other media, so that the organization does not go back to its old ways.

The 'Pure for Sure' case study (in Chapter 4) is an excellent example of *Driving Change*. Other leaders used *Driving Change* or *Team Leadership* to turn around an operation that was in deep trouble, or to make various desirable changes, such as leading the operation to become more 'outward looking' toward their customers and competition; preparing for a shift towards more open markets; becoming more performance-oriented and achieving challenging goals in terms of improving the quality of the products they provided; preparing for and executing an IPO, with all the changes that it implies; designing and producing a new high-tech version of an old standby product, with indigenous engineering.

Following the steps of change through to Level 3 or, if appropriate, Level 4 increases the chances of achieving significant and lasting success so that the change is no longer dependent on the personal efforts of the leader but becomes a part of the organizational DNA itself. This scale is different from other developmental scales in that it simultaneously represents a chronological pattern of the actions taken to implement and sustain major changes, as well as increasingly complex behavioral levels.

Although this group of the most outstanding Indian leaders is quite good at *Driving Change*, expert panels indicated that 'leading the execution' of their good ideas was a major difficulty for Indian CEOs. We surmise, going by what the expert panels had to say, that although *Driving Change* is often seen in this group of outstanding CEOs, it is *not* perceived as a

---

Box 6.2: Developmental and Chronological Levels of
Driving Change

The ability to personally lead an organization to implement and embed sustainable change.

Leads sustainable organizational change by:

1. *Embracing the change, planning implementation*
   - Identifies resistance and plans the steps and resources needed.
2. *Communicating the change, widely and constantly*
   - Articulates and demonstrates the change message, on every possible occasion, to every possible audience.
3. *Building the change into the organization*
   - Adjusts or creates organizational systems and structures to support the change.
4. *Procuring general public support to sustain the change*
   - Makes the change known to the wider community; media coverage and attention to the desired change help ensure that the organization will sustain the change.

strength in most Indian leaders—thus contributing to the much-discussed difficulties in the execution of Indian business. Another possibility is that the difficulties in timely execution of good ideas lie more in external obstacles to change than in the leaders' own ability to engage their organization in change efforts.

Empowerment with Accountability

> The CEO, with respect to his team, will have to inculcate a culture where innovation thrives and enough delegation of authority is done to make the employees feel the freedom to create and innovate.
>
> ~ **Keshub Mahindra**
> Chairman, Mahindra & Mahindra Ltd.

Finding the right balance between personally exercising leadership and delegating authority to others is a significant challenge. Outstanding CEOs recognize that not only can they not 'do it all' personally, but also that their people actually need the opportunity to take on challenges, make important decisions and even, on occasion, make mistakes. This is one of the key ways that Indian leaders develop their people's leadership competencies, as well as accomplish the work of the organization. Outstanding CEOs enable their team members to take on responsibility and deliver against challenges and adversity. They harness the human potential within their organization by identifying the capability of individuals or teams and delegating appropriate authority and responsibility to allow others to act with a sense of purpose and ownership to achieve favourable outcomes.

This competency involves blending—*not balancing*—two features: holding people accountable for performance against tasks or goals, coupled with increasing levels of trust and empowerment. By 'blending' the empowering trust with accountability, we mean that the leader does *both at the same time*. The leaders' trusting empowerment and the degree of accountability that is delegated to the team increase in tandem with each other.

Usually, the leader's relationship with an individual or group would evolve from holding people accountable with personal guidance on what to do and how to do it. Both sides work toward achieving higher levels of this competency, where the leader fully trusts and depends on his people's judgment within their areas of expertise and experience. This progression depends, of course, on the leader's assessment of the individual's or group's readiness to take on responsibility, as well as on maturity and personal willingness of the leader to share or delegate authority.

Empowerment with Accountability requires some **Inner Strength** from the leader; enabling him to trust others to make decisions without needing to exercise undue control. The leader's ability to do this (with discernment about when, with whom and under what circumstances) is a key to the

---

Box 6.3: Developmental Levels of *Empowerment with Accountability*

The maturity to delegate authority, enabling others to act with purpose and accountability.

Delegates activities with:

1. *Personal guidance and direction*
   - Tells subordinates what to do and how to do it
2. *Criteria for success*
   - Identifies what needs to be accomplished, the standards to meet, and the consequences of not meeting those standards
3. *Context for the subordinates' actions*
   - Sets the general direction and the limits within which to operate, delegating authority to decide how to do it
4. *Full autonomy*
   - Trusts his people's expertise (within certain limits) and supports their decisions

---

leader's ability to develop strength in others and, ultimately, a strong enterprise. As Keshub Mahindra recognizes, '*empowerment with authority* is one of the keys to encouraging innovation throughout the organization'.

Energizing the Team—Unique Indian Style of Accomplishing the Universal Tasks of Leadership

Though leaders of the world need to drive change in various ways, this group of Indian CEOs used a particularly clear, step-by-step style of ingraining the change in the organization. They were much less likely than Western leaders to depend on personal charisma to carry change forward. Instead, they presented their change agenda in a fairly straightforward manner (consistently over many occasions, but apparently without dramatic or emotional appeals), and followed through by making adjustments in the structure, processes or procedures of the organization, to support the desired change. This competency of *Driving Change* has no clear analogues in the generic competencies used to assess other leaders, and is qualitatively different from the patterns observed in non-Indian CEOs.

In some parts of the world, leadership is often done with a democratic-participative style (sometimes expressed as the competency of *team facilitation*), in which the leader typically solicits input from many, or all, team members in order to inform and shape decisions. In this style, the leader usually exerts influence by defining and facilitating the process by which decisions are made (often staging well-planned and well-orchestrated offsite working sessions that spread over several days or a week), rather than by personally deciding strategic direction or implementation plans. In other areas, leadership is vested in a central authority—usually the CEO—

who ultimately makes all the most important decisions and is usually treated with great respect and deference. The third style of Western leadership is the personal charisma style, which involves making inspiring speeches with an emotional impact on the audience.

The leadership styles of Indian CEOs did not fall clearly into any of these patterns. Their personal styles varied—considerably—but the pattern of behavior they used in *Driving Change* was remarkably consistent, logical, and did not clearly fall into either the democratic-participative style or the centralized-authority style. However, it would seem likely that the Indian method of *Driving Change* would be effective if it were applied elsewhere. Outstanding Indian leaders placed much less focus on how they came to a decision regarding a new direction, and much more focus on implementation.

Figure 6.1: CEOs with 'Energizing the Team' Competencies

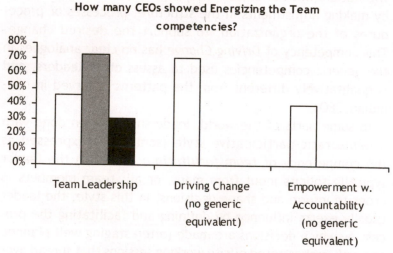

How many CEOs showed Energizing the Team competencies?

Energizing the Team competencies demonstrated at level 3 or higher in the interviews

☐ Best Indian ▨ Best International ■ Typical International

Team Leadership appears in much the same form and in similar situations in leaders worldwide. *Empowering with Accountability* relates distantly to the generic competency, *holding people accountable*, found in CEOs with moderate frequency. However, the latter is often rather punitive in tone and distinctly lacks the empowering quality that is character-istic of Indian CEOs, so that no direct comparisons can really be made. Both competencies are relatively rare—appearing in just under half of the leaders—but can make a real differ-ence in company performance when used well. Indian leaders used *Empowerment with Accountability* to help turn around operations in trouble, to find the best sources for new tech-nology; to help design new, more competitive products and to start-up new, technically challenging operations.

Internationally, leaders very often use two competencies that are strikingly absent in the stories told by even the best Indian leaders (Figure 6.2). We have presented them here

Figure 6.2: CEOs with Generic Competencies Related to Leading Teams

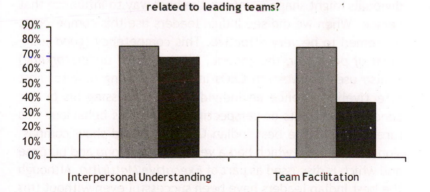

How many CEOs showed generic competencies related to leading teams?

Team Related Generic competencies demonstrated at level 3 or higher in the interviews

□ Best Indian ■ Best International ▨ Typical International

because they do appear with great consistency among CEOs in other countries, and Indian leaders might want to consider whether it would be beneficial to add these competencies to their repertoire. This may become an issue when Indian business operations become truly global, resulting in Indian leaders managing teams in other countries where employees are accustomed to this sort of behavior from their leaders. *Team facilitation*, discussed earlier in relation to *Driving Change*, is a style of leadership that engages the team discussing the decisions to be made, and actively solicits the team members' opinions and perspectives. *Interpersonal understanding*—or, as it is called in the International CEO Model, *good judgment of people*—is the other competency rarely seen in Indian CEOs. Leaders in other countries often tell about why they chose a particular person for a certain role or task, detailing the personal characteristics that made that person right for that situation. They may also consider, in detail, how an assignment would help someone grow and develop their abilities. In general, Indian leaders simply did not discuss how they matched particular people to certain roles or tasks, nor did they usually consider in detail how the personal characteristics of individuals might shape or inform the best way to influence that person. When we did see Indian leaders use this competency, it seemed to be very effective. This competency (*good judgment of people* or, the generic, *interpersonal understanding*) is also used by Western CEOs in understanding how to most effectively influence an individual by addressing his or her concerns, interests or perspective. Again, this behaviour was rarely seen in the best Indian CEOs (they did show compassionate empathy, which had a very different tone and purpose and which is discussed as part of *Executive Maturity*). Although the best Indian leaders have been successful even without this competency, we feel strongly that acquiring the ability to address the concerns and resistances of others would enhance Indian leaders' ability to mobilize people to execute strategy.

It would also be a great asset in recruiting and retaining excellent employees when competition for the best young Indian talent is becoming more intense.

Notes

1. 'Mahabharat' by Kamala Subramanian, Bhartiya Vidya Bhavan, 2004.
2. Jim Collins (2001), *Good to Great*, HarperCollins, New York.

7 Managing the Environment

The Public Sector CEO is under immense pressure from several agencies and does not have the autonomy to take actions even though he knows the needs of the customer and the market. He is answerable to far too many masters. He is inundated with requests for recruitment, transfers and promotions, which ultimately leads to the organization being burdened with additional numbers.

~**George Fernandes**
Former Minister for Defence

Today outstanding CEOs in India take personal responsibility for managing the relationship between their companies and the outside world—including other companies, the Indian government, the media and other entities. There is an increasing awareness that companies can no longer remain in a shell, confined to the narrow scope of the four walls of an organization. A constant and healthy interaction with the outside world has to happen, led by—more often than not—the man-at-the-top himself.

The three competencies in the **Managing the Environment** cluster are:

- *Networking:* The boldness to reach out to a wide network for ideas and problem solving.

- *Organizational Awareness*: The understanding of how things get decided and done in a particular organization.
- *Stakeholder Influence*: Persuasiveness, the ability to use customized strategies to influence specific stakeholders.

Although it is well understood that this is an important issue for the public sector, our data indicated that boundary management was a very significant concern for the private sector as well. In India, these relationships are especially complex and fraught with difficulties and—without the intervention of the CEO—can easily overwhelm the staff members, often interfering with their ability to accomplish other tasks. No wonder they also occupy a significant portion of the Indian CEO's attention and time.

CEOs of privately held companies had an equal number of stories on boundary management and dealing with the government as their counterparts in Public Sector Enterprises (PSEs). Such was the passion for this tricky situation and its difficulties, that many CEOs waxed eloquent about this topic in the various focus groups for this study. The huge difference between Indian leaders and their Western counterparts lies in the frequency of these difficult and frustrating situations. Indian CEOs—from both the public and private sectors—have 10 times as many of these stories to tell, compared to CEOs (or senior executives) in the West.

The bold and outgoing search for information by way of *Networking* provides the leader with not only the technological and methodological innovations needed to support **Socially Responsible Business Excellence**, but also with crucial contacts and information on managing relations with the government and the media. This information becomes part of the leaders' understanding about how these institutions operate (*Organizational Awareness*), whom to contact and how, what is possible and what is not, and what are the perspectives and concerns of those in different positions. All this allows the leader to choose the communication, the timing, and the emphasis that will be most effective (*Stakeholder Influence*).

When 'Managing the Environment' is Used Most Often

In the business environment of present times, competencies of **Managing the Environment** and, particularly, of *Organizational Awareness* and *Stakeholder Influence* come into play most often while dealing with the government and the media. The CEO is focused more on protecting his enterprise from the difficulties or distractions of boundary management, rather than on working to promote a positive interaction between the enterprise and its surrounding ecosystem. A 'let's-keep-the-devils-away' approach is often followed.

However, in other settings, or at other times, the same competencies (that the Indian CEO now devotes to boundary management) could be focused on a wide range of other issues and situations—with a positive effect.

Networking

When an Indian leader needs to know something, the preferred method of seeking information seems to be: approach someone who knows, and just ask. This is in contrast to the 'networking' common in other parts of the world. Elsewhere, 'network' could mean a web of relationships established early in life (usually at school), and used for business as well as social purposes throughout life. Or, it can mean a typically American style of deliberate and structured attempts to establish potentially—with emphasis on 'potentially'—useful relationships for less-defined business purposes. Finally, especially in parts of France and South America, 'network' refers to an intricate web of 'social' relationships within the business setting, conducted with delicacy and tact.

Today, the Indian CEO who reaches out while *Networking* usually does so with a clear and immediate business purpose in mind—and not with the quasi-social intentions that pervade business networking in some other parts of the world. Indian leaders reach out to whatever sources are likely to have useful information—even when the leader has had no previous connection or prior contact with that source of information. This bold and focused style of networking to obtain useful information from a wide variety of contacts was unique to Indian leaders. However, as Indian business expands to other countries, Indian leaders may find it helpful to consider additional forms and methods of *Networking*, in view of those practiced in other countries.

At times, the leaders sought innovative technology or the best business practices which they needed for their enterprises. *Networking*, in these cases, was paired with *Adaptive*

Box 7.1: Developmental Levels of *Networking*

The boldness to reach out to a wide network for ideas and problem solving.

Reach out for information and support:
1. *Upward—to the board, to the related ministry, etc.*
   • Maintains regular contact and two-way exchange of information
2. *Outside one's own organization*
   • Networks with competitors, suppliers, customers, other related industries, etc.
3. *Reaches out to less obvious sources*
   • Seeks ideas and input from academics, other industries, unrelated government ministries and other sources.
4. *Embassies, academics or businesses abroad*
   • Goes to other countries to gain perspective on business practices, form alliances, or joint ventures, obtain materials or equipment, or enter a distant market.

Thinking and served the purpose of technological and/or business innovation. At other times, leaders reached out to their contacts in the government, the media and elsewhere—so as to support their efforts in 'boundary management' issues, or to get assistance in obtaining permissions, or to find the best ways to address these issues. In a few instances, leaders used their contacts in the media to procure publicity to strengthen the changes they had brought about.

Organizational Awareness

> Public sector CEOs have a very difficult task indeed. They are answerable to various Committees of the Parliament which, in fact, leads to no accountability at all. Managing the Government and the Minister becomes a preoccupation.
>
> **~Subodh Bhargava**
> Advisor, Eicher Goodearth Ltd.

Organizational Awareness is the ability to imbibe, and get a feel of the inherent culture of an organization, and then engage with it in a manner that is coherent with the organization's unique style of functioning and also in a way that is perceived as politically correct. Herein comes an interesting observation; although in other settings this competency is used to understand one's own organization, or one's customers or the organizations of potential business partners, Indian CEOs generally use this competency to cope with external politics and to understand the workings of an external body, most often a government ministry.

At its best, *Organizational Awareness* enables the leader to sensitize himself to the perspectives, concerns and needs of people with whom he must deal—thus enabling him to incorporate those viewpoints into his own plans or proposals. Robust *Organizational Awareness* beefs up a leader's

Stakeholder Influence, enabling the leader to address the interests and concerns of each specific target audience. It also facilitates the development of consensus building at a variety of strategic points in the immediate business environment, like the concerned ministry for Public Sector Undertakings (PSUs). As Indian businesses become more global, and as relationships (partnerships, supplier and customer relations, joint ventures, etc.) with businesses in other countries become closer and more frequent, Indian CEOs may find it effective to apply their *Organizational Awareness* to these other companies as well.

The highest level of *Organizational Awareness*—'Understanding the organization's history and position relative to the external world'—supports the strategic thought that represents the highest level of '*adaptive thinking*'. However, the Indian leaders were often not explicit about the '*Organizational Awareness*' that supported their strategic thought,

---

Box 7.2: Developmental Levels of
Organizational Awareness

The understanding of how things get decided and done in an organization or ministry:

Understand the organization's:

1. *Formal and informal processes*
   - Knows how things normally get done in the organization—in formal processes and informal communication.
2. *Climate and culture*
   - Sees how unspoken organizational culture impacts the way work is perceived and accomplished, and how communication or some such action affects the organization.
3. *Power structure and decision making*
   - Recognizes and predicts the impact of power and political relationships—who will help or hinder an initiative, and why.
4. *Ongoing and underlying issues*
   - Understands how external factors, internal history, and other factors affect the organization's ongoing behavior and structure—and the implications for change.

perhaps because they focused more on 'What does India need?' rather than on 'What are the potentials of the organization in the market?'

Stakeholder Influence

Communication with all the stakeholders is an important element of the CEO's task.

~**Rajendra Singh**
Ex-CMD, NTPC, and Chairman,
Mumbai Integrated Special Economic Zone Ltd.

'The art of getting things done by others' is one of the simplest definitions of leadership. So, as a corollary to this simple definition, the ability to persuade or to influence others is a key skill in the repertoire of a successful leader. This task—when seen from the leader's point of view—often appears in the form of the **Energizing the Team** competencies, while working within the sphere of one's own organization. If the leader is attempting to extend his sphere of influence outside his own organization, then the competency used is *Stakeholder Influence*.

Stakeholder Influence is most effective when the approach used is customized to a specific audience, keeping aside the 'one-size-fits-all' approach. Moreover, this does not mean tinkering with the message itself, but establishing a connection with the audience by using the language, logic and emphasis on topics that would go down well with that particular set of people.

It is a tricky task, often including finer issues of leadership—like sensitivity pertaining to correct timing, when and how hard to push, and when to back off. These are small observations, yet important enough to be kept in mind. As the leader customizes his language and actions, it is important that the leader maintains sincerity and genuine conviction in choosing the most relevant message as well as the most effective way to get the point across—so that the leader comes across as a genuine person and not a glib talker that many leaders are perceived to be.

Effective *Stakeholder Influence* means that the leader has tuned in to, and comprehended, his audience's perspective and concerns, having fully understood their told and untold agendas. This understanding of the other's interest and perspectives can come from *interpersonal understanding* of the other individual (a competency noticeably missing in our sample of outstanding CEOs), or from *Organizational Awareness*, which is the supporting competency most often found in this group. At the higher levels, *Stakeholder Influence* can include more complex strategies comprising a number of customized communications aimed at different individuals or groups, spread over time and a variety of settings.

Box 7.3: *Stakeholder Influence*

Persuasiveness, the ability to use customised strategies to influence specific stakeholders.

Influence others by using:

1. *Direct persuasion*
   - Uses logical and rational arguments, supported by data.
2. *Words and actions customized to the audience*
   - Uses an understanding of the audience, its concerns and perspectives, to choose the words or actions that will most appeal to or affect that audience.
3. *Indirect Influence*
   - Builds behind-the-scene support to ensure buy-in and ownership;
   - Undertakes suitable groundwork and covers 'all the bases' before addressing powerful or important audiences.
4. *Complex influence strategies*
   - Carefully plans and implements complex influence strategies;
   - Creates external conditions wherein business can flourish.

Managing the Environment: Indian Leaders Use Similar Skills for Purposes Different from their Western Counterparts

Apart from thinking, planning and engaging the energy and commitment of the team, the leader also has the task of managing the boundaries between the enterprise and the surrounding world. Although the routine aspects of this role are delegated to others (sales-people, customer contact people, purchasers, etc.), the most important and strategic aspects of this role belong to the Chief Executive. While this is true across the world, in India this role of boundary management takes on a unique importance along with unique forms, and occupies a much more time-consuming and central role than in other countries.

Indian leaders seem to spend *far* more time and energy (compared to leaders in many other countries) in managing relationships with governmental agencies and, to a slightly lesser extent, the fourth estate. They have to respond to inquiries and investigations and, sometimes even face pressures to take decisions in one direction or another. More often than not, they must *personally* make efforts to get licenses and permissions for many activities. While these functions exist in other parts of the world, getting permissions and licenses in those places is usually a routine matter handled lower in the organization. In the HayGroup database, we observe that in the United States it is mostly in health care and oil industries that high-level executives are often personally involved in regulatory matters. Even in these industries, these matters may be handled by Vice Presidents or even by professional lobbyists, rather than by the CEO personally.

Organizational Awareness here is very similar to what is seen in leaders across the world. Yet, while in Indian leaders it is more focused towards understanding the organization of the government, leaders elsewhere are more focused towards understanding commercial organizations—their own as well as others'.

In India, *Stakeholder Influence* was mostly seen in relation to influencing the government to obtain licenses or permissions. Leaders in other countries use similar behaviors more often (per leader) *and* in a wider variety of settings: to influence individuals within one's own company or in other companies with which one has commercial dealings. Leaders in other countries use their understanding of specific individuals, their concerns, preferences and perspectives *(interpersonal understanding)* to enhance their ability to influence those individuals (*Stakeholder Influence*, or the related generic competency of *impact and influence*). In India, *Stakeholder Influence* was generally supported and shaped by *Organizational Awareness* rather than by individual *interpersonal understanding*.

Leaders in other countries use the competencies of *Organizational Awareness* and *Stakeholder Influence* more frequently, and for purposes different from those of their Indian counterparts, that is, to gain internal consensus, sometimes in relations with a board of directors, in dealing with the most important customers, in negotiation of joint ventures and alliances, sometimes in influencing industry organizations, and only occasionally in dealing with the government or the media.

Indian executives are extraordinarily bold in seeking out information—be it in India or any other source globally—and processing it to strengthen their own organizations. The best part is that they do more information seeking through personal contacts and *Networking* than their global counterparts. Compared to CEOs in other countries, Indian CEOs are more likely to use networks of contacts to gather information and are more likely to contact people directly, while other leaders are more likely to use journals, business news and other sources of information. Sometimes, leaders in other countries also use their networks of contacts (the competency of *relationship building*) for a variety of other purposes—to improve the reputation of their enterprise, for joint ventures or alliances, to get contracts, etc.—and only occasionally to gain information.

In India, *Networking* activities appear to be driven primarily by a focus on the business task rather than by an interest in influencing others or establishing friendly, positive relationships.

Networking is compared to two different generic competencies namely, *information seeking* and *relationship building* (Figure 7.1) because it combines these generic competencies in a unique configuration. Indian leaders, it has been observed, use their unique combination of *information seeking* and r*elationship building,* more often than Western leaders use either competency.

While the Indian methods of 'managing the boundaries' are very well adapted to the Indian situation, Indian CEOs may find it useful to broaden their repertoire of *Networking* and *Stakeholder Influence* skills when they expand their operations into other countries. Conversely, when Western business leaders do business in India, they will find it useful to understand how relationships and influence operate here.

Figure 7.1: CEOs with 'Managing the Environment' Competencies

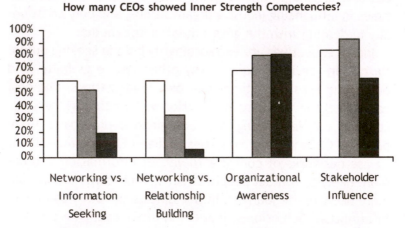

How many CEOs showed Inner Strength Competencies?

Managing the Environment competencies at level 2 or higher, or generic equivalent demonstrated in the interviews

☐ Best Indian ▨ Best International ■ Typical International

8 | Inner Strength

> Value-based leadership and a culture that promotes integrity are the most important elements which the CEO has the responsibility to inculcate. The CEO should build passion around the goals of the organization and bond the team through sustaining values.
>
> **~ P.M. Sinha**
> Ex-CEO, Pepsico India

Inner Strength provides a moral compass to the leader as well as to the organization. Like a lighthouse it guides both the leader and his company through turbulent waters (when ships have been known to sink hard and fast)—in the face of difficult decisions, moral dilemmas and complex problems—not only on a personal level but also on the professional one. Being a CEO is a tough job, one in which both personal strengths and personal weaknesses might emerge under pressure.

The two **Inner Strength** competencies are:

- *Executive Maturity:* Emotional wisdom to respond to others and to embody the values and aspirations of the organization.
- *Transcending Self:* Courageous dedication to super-ordinate goals; to do what is right and what would make India great.

The sense of purpose in *Transcending Self* provides motivation to continue the struggle despite all difficulties; while *Executive Maturity* helps the leader to channel his energy wisely, enabling him to help and inspire others. Those people who recognize a leader's **Inner Strength** (and generally they *do*, no matter how modest the leader) feel inspired; it evokes in them a sense of loyalty and commitment to work towards the goals set by the leader. **Inner Strength** also plays a most significant role in establishing a critical aspect of leadership—the personal credibility of the leader.

Understandably, many leaders from a wide spectrum of religious backgrounds found a source of **Inner Strength** in their respective faiths—though many others also found *non*-religious sources of strength. The Indian leaders often discussed their sources of support *in the middle of their stories* about difficult situations. This is in strong contrast to leaders from other countries who rarely mention such sources of strength as part of their work stories, even though they may have similar sources of strength in their personal lives. The outstanding Indian leaders who *did* talk about their faith found in it a source of courage that empowered their decision-making and helped them build their businesses and contribute towards building the Indian economy. However, they did *not* use their business or economic power to support a sectarian religious agenda. Leaders who truly found personal strength in their faith also showed tolerance and respect for other faiths (e.g. providing, before meetings, the time for a silent prayer or reflection, thus giving everyone a certain level of comfort in participating).

When Inner Strength is the Most Important

The leader's own **Inner Strength** is especially important during start-ups and in turnarounds—in particularly testing and stressful times when an inner lighthouse is needed most. In the leadership journey, CEOs sometimes even engage in a particular start-up or turnaround situation because it is for the larger good of the country and its economy, their motives in such cases transcending even the financial and economic benefits for the firm.

It is striking how the needs of India's population were often provided as a reason to undertake a particularly difficult or risky business enterprise or, for that matter, to persist against seemingly overwhelming odds. Leaders spoke freely of the poor people's need for a salt that would retain its iodine content given their cooking methods; watches that were inexpensive yet reliable; goods and fuels that were unadulterated; vehicles that were not only affordable but would also adapt to their particular needs and terrain; or the need for more Indians to be able to purchase their own homes. Leaders realized that certain industries/utilities are necessary to support the overall growth of the country's economy—for high-tech industries to provide jobs and help curtail the brain-drain of some of India's brightest graduates. These comments were not merely assertions of a value for India's development. Instead, leaders offered these comments as the basis to explain specific difficult and critical business decisions. These outstanding leaders do not just talk about the importance of serving the nation; they make this value an intrinsic part of their business thought process.

When leaders lobby with the government, **Inner Strength** often stands out as the factor differentiating between success and frustration. It is possible that government officials sense the very sincerity of the leader's purpose—in helping empower India—and, therefore, are more favourable towards them. Certainly, a leader needs *Executive Maturity* to deal with the delay, stress and frustration in the process, as much as to motivate his/her own team.

Executive Maturity

> It is personal courage and conviction on the part of the CEO which leads him to success.
>
> ~**V.N. Kaul**
> Comptroller and Auditor General of India

Executive Maturity is the appropriate combination of maturity and strength of character required to lead from the front. The practical side of emotional intelligence, this competency enables a leader to control his/her emotions and, thereby, to control the effect of these on others. It begins with the leader being in tune with his inner self—fully aware of his own reactions and what causes them. Only when the leader understands the cause, can the leader control the effect, that is, learn to manage his/her own feelings, energy level, emotional state and reactions to the same. Once a leader is internally in synch, it becomes increasingly easier to 'connect' with others.

The extremely stressful nature of today's leadership underlines the need to manage one's own motivation and stamina. However, *Executive Maturity* can be developed further to include both the ability to understand and to respond in a positive and compassionate manner, thus inspiring others to perform well even when circumstances are trying. We saw outstanding leaders who set an example of personal valour in difficult or dangerous situations (such as natural catastrophes) and, at the same time, showed their compassion for the practical and emotional difficulties their people experienced, doing what they could to alleviate or—at least—share the difficulties. Other leaders exhibited enormous patience, good temper and stamina during prolonged negotiations that lasted late into the night. Their calm demeanours contributed greatly to the eventually satisfactory conclusions to the negotiations.

Executive Maturity has a tone of realistic resilience (facing and acknowledging difficulties honestly, without being overcome by them) and of compassionate understanding—both toward oneself and toward others. It is a secret *mantra* many leaders fail to understand, but one on which these outstanding Indian leaders unfailingly rely.

Box 8.1: Developmental Levels of *Executive Maturity*

Emotional wisdom to respond to others and to embody the aspirations of the organization.

Visible personal maturity in the area of:

1. *Emotional Self Awareness*
   - Is aware of own emotional reactions, and what causes them
2. *Self-Management*
   - Uses personal strategies and resources to manage own reactions and provide a source of strength and resilience
3. *Empathy—tuning in to others*
   - Responds to others with compassionate understanding
4. *Embodying the aspirations and values of the organization*
   - Models maturity and composure in dealing with challenging or stressful situations.
   - Personifies the organization's ideals and values in the leader's behavior and demeanor

---

Transcending Self

In all the major decisions that I have taken, I have been guided by an inner voice.

~D.S. Brar
Former CEO/MD, Ranbaxy Laboratories Ltd.

In *Transcending Self*, the leader shows courage and dedication in working towards a higher purpose—going beyond both his career and the success of his business—to act upon a conviction rooted in universal human values, or his concern for the overall benefit of society and his belief in the idea of

India's greatness. These values (that transcend self-interest or even the limited interests of the enterprise) and this dedication are what enable the leader to do right (right for India as a nation usually or, sometimes, right in view of a more humane good) even in difficult situations; overcoming obstacles, difficulties or personal risks. This higher goal helps organize and motivate the leader's plans as well as the risks that are chosen.

In order to think about and apply this competency, it is essential that leaders consider what is actually best for India in the long run. Their actions, then, tend to ensure that critical technologies, industries or capacities are developed in India while supporting the growth of a more productive economy. At times, a tough decision to lay off an unproductive portion of a company's workforce—in order to make the enterprise productive and viable on the whole—could be an example of this competency. We did occasionally observe this scenario.

What struck us was how closely the concerns of today's most outstanding Indian business leaders matched the thought pattern observed by Manohar Nadkarni[1] (when he conducted follow-up visits and interviews with small entrepreneurs who had participated in the Achievement Motivation courses led by David McClelland) in the 1960s. Nadkarni's description of the entrepreneurs' thoughts applies beautifully to our observations in this study:

> The nature of their achievement imagery had also changed.... Before the course, they had nearly all seen business success as being almost wholly materialistic and selfish. Thus they were somewhat ambivalent about pursuing it too seriously. In their hearts, many of them agreed with Chaudhuri that the pursuit of money is shameful at the highest moral level. It is best to do one's duty, if one's *dharma* is business, but not to pursue it too vigorously, since that would be a sign of selfishness and disregard for higher values in life, such as serving others. After the course more of the men saw increased business activity not primarily as a selfish way of making more money, but as a way to develop the whole community and ultimately, India. Thus Shri Nadkarni found that when they talked about doing something in business, they nearly always coupled

it with the notion that they were doing something for the community. Some critics may regard this new stance as hypocritical, as a cover for their increased greed. But the critic would have to admit that a repeated expressed concern for the welfare of the community as a personal achievement goal is better than no such expressed concern. And in fact, in many cases it seemed to be leading men away from activities which would gain them more money more quickly (e.g. as in traditional money-lending) and toward more risky, long-term investments in industry, because industry would provide more employment in the town.

Even today, the best Indian leaders do exactly that: they take more, or bigger, business risks *so as to provide something that India needs in order to be great*. When leaders were deciding to start a risky new venture—and persisting against all obstacles—whether expanding the range of financial services available to Indian householders, investing in oil fields, designing a much better new product, entrusting key sourcing decisions to their subordinates or investing time and resources to

---

Box 8.2: Developmental Levels of *Transcending Self*

Courageous dedication to super-ordinate goals: doing what is right and what will make India great

Dedication to doing what is right in:

1. *Making decisions*
   - Makes business decisions—or inspire others—based on what is in the best interest of India.
2. *Doing the right thing when it's not easy*
   - Acts on a belief in India's local abilities; provides support to realize that potential.
   - Acts ethically, promoting ethics in the organization.
3. *Persisting against obstacles*
   - Continues to work for the overall good; taking business risks, against obstacles, discouragement and difficulties.
   - Shares resources on projects for the public good—for their own sake.
4. *Displaying Courage*
   - Takes serious personal or career risks to do the right thing or what will make India grow.

---

significantly improve the quality of their products, the impact of the new or expanded venture on India's overall development and greatness was usually mentioned as a reason to take this risk. Leaders said they took these decisions 'because India needs this to become great', or 'without this, India cannot grow as well or as fast'. It was very clear to us that these leaders would not have made the same efforts or taken the same risks just to make money from a venture that they did not see as significantly contributing to India's overall wellbeing. And this is something we simply have not seen elsewhere.

Inner Strength: Indian Leaders Excel, Compared to Leaders in Other Countries

The **Inner Strength** of Indian CEOs was striking in its intensity and in its unique focus on what was best for India. The focus on a higher purpose in *Transcending Self* relates to a more diffused sense of *social responsibility* sometimes seen in CEOs in other countries. The Indian leaders are unique both in the intensity of this quality and its national focus. This competency also relates to the generic competency of *integrity* (doing what is right at some cost or risk) seen in the best executives in other countries. The Indian CEOs show this characteristic at significantly higher levels than do their international counterparts.

Executive Maturity contains elements of *emotional intelligence* that are much discussed—but not always observed—in the West. It also contains some elements of *interpersonal understanding*, one of the generic competencies seen in many roles around the world. However, the empathy found in *Executive Maturity* is directed toward groups rather than individuals, and it has a tone of genuineness, and of compassionate response (and a lack of instrumental purpose), that is missing in the competency of *interpersonal understanding*. Western leaders use *interpersonal understanding* to evaluate individuals regarding their likelihood of success given particular tasks or roles, or in terms of how to influence them effectively and rarely, if ever, in the context of responding compassionately to the natural feelings of groups of people. This fundamental difference in purpose and approach, plus the other aspects of *Executive Maturity* that make it a source of **Inner Strength** to the leaders themselves, make a statistical comparison between *Executive Maturity* and *interpersonal understanding* inappropriate. Therefore, there is no direct statistical comparison regarding *Executive Maturity* between the Indian CEOs and their Western counterparts.

It seems that being an outstanding leader in India requires enormous personal strength. This is probably due to the unusual difficulties attached to business leadership in India. While it is inspiring and impressive that India has produced leaders with so much **Inner Strength**, perhaps the country's economic

Figure 8.1: CEOs with 'Inner Strength' Competencies

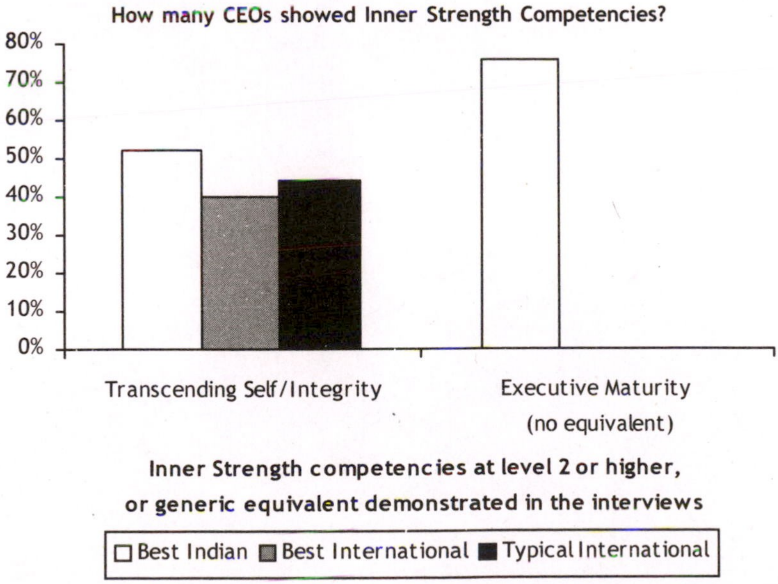

How many CEOs showed Inner Strength Competencies?

Inner Strength competencies at level 2 or higher,
or generic equivalent demonstrated in the interviews

☐ Best Indian ▨ Best International ■ Typical International

development would be better served if a way could be found to make business leadership a little less difficult. We are particularly concerned that, in addition to the financial and career risks that necessarily accompany entrepreneurial endeavours, some leaders also faced intimidation and threats of personal harm. Just as it was wrong—and detrimental to economic development—for Western business leaders to use threats and intimidation against unions in the 19th and early 20th centuries, it is equally wrong—and detrimental to economic development—for Indian management leaders to be intimidated or threatened by any vested interests.

Note

1. D.C. McClelland, David Winter, Sarah Winter, Elliot Danzig, Manohar Nadkarni, Aziz Pabaney and Udai Pareek (1979), *Motivating Economic Achievement*, Free Press, New York.

II

What Makes a CEO Successful?

II

9   In a Turnaround Situation

The Question

When selecting the CEO, should the business situation of the company be taken into account?

If so, what characteristics would be most helpful in certain situations?

Are certain competencies especially important in certain situations: for example, a turnaround as compared to one that is launching new products or services?

These questions, put forth by the Public Enterprise Selection Board (PESB), are answered in this chapter and in Chapters 10-12. The PESB sensed that CEOs need to behave differently in different situations, and that the qualities they would look for in a CEO for a failing business would have to differ from a CEO for a business expecting incremental growth. If we could identify the patterns of competencies that led to success in key situations, those patterns could be used for more focused selection, and could also provide a guide to CEOs facing such situations.

To begin with, we turned to the *stories* told to us in the Behavioral Event Interviews (BEIs) of 30 most outstanding

Indian CEOs. Each interview comprised two to four, in-depth stories about recent, key events in the CEO's work-life, along with the outcomes to these events. Each CEO had a free choice about what stories to tell; we simply asked for times they felt effective and for times that were more frustrating. The leaders generously offered details about what they did and said, and about what they were thinking and feeling, in the course of these situations.

For every story told to us by one of the CEOs, we asked ourselves a very simple question: 'What is this story all about?' Stories with similar answers to this simple question were **grouped**—all the turnarounds, all the start-ups (launching a new product or service or factory), and so on. This grouping was done quite empirically, using the descriptions the leaders themselves provided, allowing each group of stories to be as big or as small as it happened to be. Fortunately, there were sufficient stories provided to address the three key situations about which the PESB had asked.

Most of the stories told by the Indian CEOs fell into four **groups**:

(1) *Turnarounds*: moving an existing business from significantly losing money to making money.
(2) *Start-ups*: starting a new business, a new product line, a new operation or a very large project.
(3) *Improving existing business*: attempting to change the culture, or to re-organize the enterprise, or to introduce new technology, or to improve the company's position through marketing or re-branding the products.
(4) *Dealing with the government*: efforts to obtain various licenses, permissions and, occasionally, changes in regulation.

There were a few other types of scenarios, where we did not have enough stories of the same **group** to make an analysis. These relatively rare **groups** of stories included:

- finding or changing strategic direction (these were events where the new strategic direction had not yet been implemented at the time of the interview);
- raising capital investments in the enterprise (these were from the private sector);
- looking for strategic partners, or joint ventures;
- working to give something back to India as a whole— through various charitable or developmental initiatives, sharing what the CEO had learned in his own business with the rest of India Inc.

We hope that additional research will discover what Indian business leaders do to be effective in these situations (as well as in the four groups of stories we discuss here). As time and research go on, additional strategic situations may emerge.

It was striking that the vast majority of the outstanding Indian leader's stories were *directly* concerned with increasing the profitability and/or growth of their enterprises, whereas leaders in other countries are also concerned with matters of prestige, reputation, internal politics (other than performance improvements) and other matters not directly related to performance or growth.

Strategic Situation Analysis Methods

We previously identified specific Indian CEO competencies— with a general description and specific behaviors arranged in developmental scales from easier (Level 1) to the most advanced and difficult (Level 4). These competencies are arranged in four 'clusters' or groups of related or similar competencies (refer to Figure 3.1). These competencies—their definitions, including the behaviours—are described in the previous chapters. The Indian CEO competencies were developed by grouping similar behaviors (thoughts, feelings, speeches, decisions and actions) described by the leaders in their stories—in other words, by identifying the 'atoms' of behavior that repeatedly occurred in this group of the most outstanding Indian business leaders (and which do not often occur in typical business leaders worldwide). Having identified these specific atoms of behaviour, it was time to explore how these could fit together in specific contexts.

> We re-read each story in order to identify specific competencies, demonstrated with a convincing amount of detail. For each story, we thus developed a profile of the specific actions, thought patterns and feelings the leader used in the course of that event/situation. Considering that we 'counted' only the thoughts, actions, etc., which were described as having actually occurred in the course of an event, we are using a very conservative measure of competencies. *Although it is possible that the leaders used additional competencies, we can be sure that the competencies identified by this process were present.*

Within each **group** of stories (turnarounds, start-ups, improving existing businesses, dealing with the government), we:

- **looked at the results** that the leaders (and their teams) achieved, and
- **sorted the stories** according to the more successful and the less successful.

We collected a helpful range of outcomes because we asked for stories that the interviewee saw as 'high points' (they felt effective, and were successful) and 'low points' (things did not go so well despite their efforts, and they were not so successful), and because the participants were frank and generous in discussing both types of situations/events. Specific outcomes, that were considered more successful or less successful, are described in the discussion of each type of situation. At times, the same leader had two stories **in the same group**—two turnarounds or two different start-ups—one story about a more successful event and the other about a less successful one.

Having grouped the stories according to the main subject (e.g., turnaround, start-up, etc), we next compared the competencies used in the more effective stories with those used in the partly effective stories *in the same group*. We looked for three **patterns** of competencies:

- **Crucial:** 'Crucial' competencies are those that were used in the *majority* of events in a group (both the most successful and the less successful). Competencies were considered 'crucial' if they appeared in at least 75 per cent of the events.
- **Added Value:** These competencies or clusters of competencies were more noticeable in stories with the best outcomes, but less or not at all noticeable in those with less successful outcomes. These competencies are reasonably assumed to contribute to the success of these events.
- **Counter-productive:** These competencies were associated with *less-effective* outcomes in one group of stories (i.e., one type of situation). The behaviours included in 'counter-productive' competencies may actually hinder success in the type of situation in which they are 'counter-productive', even though the very same competencies and behaviours are crucial or add value in a different group of situations.

Box 9.1: Formula for Success in a Turnaround

Most stories, as told by Indian CEOs, included the competency of:

- *Transcending Self* (also referred to as 'contributing to making India great', sometimes with personal courage) and/or *Executive Maturity* to sustain the energy and commitment of the leader in the face of difficulties.
- *Excellence in Execution* (unfailing and persevering focus on taking action) and/or *Entrepreneurial Drive* (a spirit of entrepreneurship and competitiveness, based on challenging, world-class goals,

---

Box 9.1 contd.

Box 9.1 contd.

and on an energetic pursuit of a detailed vision of a better future).
- *Driving Change* (planning, communicating and building it into the organization) and/or *Empowerment with Accountability* (enabling others in the organization to act with purpose and accountability).

For real success, also include:

- The highest levels of *Adaptive Thinking* to re-structure the enterprise's strategic direction—to include new markets, new products, new distribution channels or other strategic changes that enabled a sustained level of profitability.

Box 9.2: How to Read the 'Formula for Success'

The **first** part of the formula (i.e. 'Most stories, as told by Indian CEOs ...') lists the 'crucial' competencies that appeared in at least 75 per cent of the stories. We consistently found these competencies in both more and less successful events.

The **second** part (i.e. 'For real success ...') comprises those competencies that appeared *only*—or almost only—in the most successful events. These are the 'added value' competencies.

The **third** part (i.e. 'Avoid this...') comprises those competencies that appeared *only*—or almost only—in the less successful events, the 'counterproductive' competencies.

So, based on the evidence in the collection of stories provided by the CEOs, we would advise leaders to be sure to do the competencies in the 'most stories include' *and* the 'for real success' sections, and to avoid, in this situation, the 'avoid this' competency, if there is one.

However, these formulas should be read as *minimum* requirements: in any particular event, the leader interviewed may have used additional competencies that were specific to the needs of that event but not part of a consistent general pattern. In real-life situations, a leader may need to use additional competencies, even ones not described in this model.

Competencies for Turning-around a Business

These stories spoke of how a leader came to a company or an operation that was in deep trouble, losing money and in danger of failing altogether, and what the leader then did. The leader's main goal was to put the enterprise back on a solid footing so that it not only stops losing money but actually starts making profit, as well as providing a sound basis for continued profits in the future. These situations are the most challenging and require the broadest range of competencies.

Generally, the leader who turns a company around is different from the one present when the company got into trouble. In that sense, he is new to the situation/company notwithstanding extensive leadership experience elsewhere. A variety of factors were responsible for the troubles described in these stories: change in the markets, new competition, slow decline in sales or efficiency, difficult labor relations that impeded production, and so on. Often, one of the first things a leader had to do—after stepping into the shoes of the former CEO—was to identify the root cause of the trouble.

The BEIs provided 12 stories of turnarounds: five 'most successful' and seven 'partly successful'. In case of the former, leaders provided details of how the '*operation has now achieved and sustained a solidly profitable status*'. Here, the CEO generally provided some financial figures regarding the then current profitability of the operation. In case of the latter, progress had been made and the operation was approaching— or had achieved—a breakeven position, but was not actually making profits yet, or the financial outcome was still unclear. In either case, there was no clear indication of failure in a turnaround situation (surely such stories existed, but were not spoken about by this sample of truly outstanding leaders).

Turnarounds are among the most difficult and challenging situations that a leader can face often combining competitive challenges, difficulties with employees, technological changes and market changes, all under the pressure of time and limited resources. The number, sophistication and range of competencies in all the stories are truly impressive. Although some turnaround situations called for dealings with the government (for permissions, etc.), leaders treated this as a separate event. Following the lead of our participants, we have analyzed the stories about such dealings (with the government and/or media) separately.

During a turnaround, most outstanding leaders used the competencies from the following three clusters:

1. **Socially Responsible Business Excellence:** To identify and resolve business problems and to define the course of action for the company.
2. **Energizing the Team:** To engage and energize the entire team and their energies, creativity and innovation and to make changes in the organization for it to sustain.
3. **Inner Strength:** To focus the company's energies on a direction that would benefit India as well as the company itself and to provide inner resources to sustain the leader through very difficult period(s).

During turnarounds, the leaders did *not consistently* use the competencies of **Managing the Environment**—with the exception of *Networking* to gather innovations and ideas that would help resolve business problems. We also did not come across counter-productive ('avoid this') competencies in the turnaround scenarios.

While leaders certainly need to 'stem the bleeding' quickly, doing so is not enough to ensure a complete and lasting turnaround. They must also address the underlying problems that led to the situation in the first place. In general, in an era of swift and increasing competition, this means finding a new strategy (sometimes new products or markets, at other times better adapted technology, a new business model and focus on certain areas of business while cutting back on those the company cannot manage as well). This strategic re-focusing (the most sophisticated and complete version *Adaptive Thinking*—Level 4: coming to a new strategic insight) appears in four out of the five most successful turnarounds, the ones where the leader could cite the profitability of the turned around operation, but in only one of the seven partly successful turnaround stories.

In many cases *Adaptive Thinking* was supported by *Networking*—to gather the ideas and information that shaped the new strategy. Sometimes, the best leaders went abroad to gather the best practices, new technologies and ideas that would help save their operation. But they did not stop with learning what other companies, in other countries were doing—they changed and adapted the technology or the ideas to fit their company's needs and to support a whole new strategy. In other cases, the leaders went to their own customers and operations to find out the cause beneath the problems.

> One leader, who was faced with a severe drop in demand for his product as well as rising inventories, went with his Marketing Director on a two-week tour to meet his distributors and consumers 'just to understand what my customers say and why they are not buying it. I wanted to understand, very simply, what is the customer's issue (networking).
>
> He discovered, to his dismay, that the customers had many complaints about the quality and reliability of the product. 'And that woke me up and I realized if I want to succeed, I have to upgrade the quality and this changed my total game plan.' And he went on from that to transforming his enterprise's entire approach to quality. His revised approach aimed at dramatically improving the quality of the product and thus attaining a new, much more successful position in the market.

Another leader recognized that in his industry, continual technological improvement—along with cost reduction—was the key to success. He learned methods from leading US companies. He also radically reorganized the company, reducing resources in some areas and re-launching the R&D department with more resources and a new emphasis.

> So when I was interacting with the senior management of ABC (a very successful US company), who came here for discussions about setting up a joint venture. I was trying to talk to them and understand their good practices. One thing that appealed to me during this discussion was a practice of continuous cost reduction that they followed in the US. I told them that my objective of setting up a joint venture is just not in the interest of establishing a new entity, but also to learn from you as you are a global company that is doing very well. So this appealed to me.
>
> – *Networking*—against world-class benchmarks

Once the problems were clearly identified, the leaders devised strategies to address the problems and to re-position their company and products in the marketplace. They found new markets for their products. They made significant innovations in manufacturing processes to produce much higher quality goods at about the same price, enabling them now to compete on the basis of high quality, or to reduce the cost for the same level of quality. In each case, these changes were not made randomly, but were part of a well-thought-through and coordinated strategy, which involved significant organizational culture change to support and sustain the new strategic focus.

While the highest levels of *Adaptive Thinking* seem to be necessary for a fully successful turnaround, just changing the business model or the strategy is not enough. The leader needs to build that change into the organization, to 'execute' the plan. In a turnaround, good execution requires many different competencies from the leader, all working together.

In attempting to turnaround a company that is in trouble, the leader needs to draw on **Inner Strength**. A turnaround is a long, difficult task, often with daunting challenges and complexities. If the leader lacks personal strength, the task may prove very difficult. Indian CEOs often drew courage to take business and personal risks from their belief in the importance of their enterprise to the strength and growth of India as a country (*Transcending Self*).

A typical explanation for persisting in a seemingly hopeless situation was:

> I couldn't let this fail, because India needed [this industry], needed to have this available to support economic development.

For some leaders, their personal faith was a source of strength, for themselves and even for others. This was true for leaders from a variety of faiths, although other CEOs also found strength from a variety of non-religious sources.

On the first day, I prayed before I went to meet with the Board. Instead of starting with a drink, as each one of them did, I started the Board meeting with a moment of silent prayer, [so each board member could pray according to their own faith]. That started the change in the culture and the attitudes. I was telling them, 'Look, we have to change our ways. If you want to have improvement, then you have to start with us, at the top. There's no point in blaming the people below. We have to set the example'

The CEO's *Executive Maturity* was often called upon for stamina in dealing with difficult negotiations or with the sheer amount of effort necessary to make the required changes in the enterprise in a relatively short time. Although in the West turnarounds often involve significant numbers of lay-offs both in the management ranks (as they are seen as the source of the problem) and in the ranks of the workers (in order to reduce costs) the Indian leaders most often accomplished their turnarounds with essentially the same personnel. In order to do this they used a remarkable level of *Executive Maturity* to listen to their 'opponents' with compassion and faith.

I came into this enterprise in which a little scare had built up with time [the previous leaders had been driven away by aggressive labour]. On my asking about the groups in the company that opposed a new leader, I got a list of about ten groups that were 'undisciplined, very apprehensive and very volatile.' I smilingly said, 'Okay, I will have a one-to-one talk with each of these groups within 48 hours and will ask them what are their apprehensions, what they want, why they are opposing, where is their stake and what is good for them?' It was my gut feeling that I can convince them that I will do what is good for them. My conviction has been that employees can understand that their interest ultimately depends on the company's good. If the company is not doing well then they too would not benefit...as they are wage earners. They want to have peace, they want to see prosperity for the company and they also understand that their prosperity comes with the company's prosperity. [After these meetings, in which this leader simply listened with an open heart, he returned home to find his doorway heaped with flowers sent by employees who were grateful to him as he heard them all with understanding and compassion.]

The CEO's own **Inner Strength** is just the beginning. It must be combined with clear-headed business thinking (the **Socially Responsible Business Excellence** competencies, particularly *Excellence in Execution* and/or *Entrepreneurial Drive*). Turnarounds require enormous energy and drive from the leader. Often this appears as a sense of urgency in addressing the critical problems and persistence against the many obstacles and difficulties (*Excellence in Execution*). Leaders also show a strong dedication to establish and meet very specific and challenging goals ('reduce costs by 10 percent not 1 per cent' or 'have this new technology operational by _____') and an understanding of both the potential costs and benefits of a course of action, balancing costs and benefits against each other to find the best way forward (*Entrepreneurial Drive*).

But the CEO is not in the enterprise alone; the entire organization must be brought into the change. Even the best business plans are not effective until they are instilled into the team through the **Energizing the Team** competencies, particularly *Driving Change* and/or *Empowerment with Accountability*, and become an ongoing and permanent part of the organization. Often, especially in the most successful stories, the leader starts with his own entrepreneurial drive and his own sense of urgency, but then finds ways to evoke the same feelings in his team so that the energy for change is coming from them, and not only from him. The leader may provide the general direction and the challenging goals and then empower his team to think of the details of how to achieve those goals through *Empowerment with Accountability*.

In effective turnarounds, behaviours from **Energizing the Team** and **Socially Responsible Business Excellence** can be so interwoven that you can hardly see one without the other. The story below illustrates how one leader wove his own passion for action and entrepreneurship into his leadership, during a crucial turnaround:

[First he went around to meet with groups of people quite a bit lower in the organization, asking for their perceptions and their experiences. He said] 'many of the issues raised by them were valid and therefore needed to be addressed.

~ Executive Maturity

But I didn't want it to be only problem solving, I wanted to throw in a challenge as well. I told them, 'Okay, I will make a timetable to correct this and then will come back to you to tell you about the things we have solved. But at the same time you people have a certain responsibility.' I painted the picture that 'we are going very badly, we are really slow to respond and as a result we are losing ground. We seem to be very inward looking; we are not seeing how things outside have already changed. This arrogance of success we have in us is not letting us realize that other people can help us solve the problems. We have to get out of this and you have a certain role in making it happen.'

~ beginning of Driving Change

So they were all enthused by that because they wanted to do something. I said, 'Look, my first priority is cost reduction.' And we had been talking about cost reductions of half per cent to quarter of a per cent per annum. I said to them, 'We need to talk about huge cost reductions. I'm saying it has to be at least 10 per cent for this year.' In the context of the industry that is not outlandish but in the internal context, going from half per cent to 10 per cent makes you think very differently. You will try to stretch then. Because if you think of 1 per cent, you will never reach 10 per cent, but if you say 10 per cent then you begin to think in a way that is totally out of the box. And you find you come with suggestions which you would not have otherwise have thought of.

~ Entrepreneurial Drive—in pursuit of excellence

So I asked these people who were from different disciplines, and told them, 'Look, come back in four hours and I want to see a presentation from you on how you could reduce costs by 10 per cent.' (This was so that they could put their heads together, seeing this as an organizational issue which needed everyone's involvement so as to work towards a common agenda.) Then they came back in the afternoon, and I must say it was an absolutely fascinating presentation. Following that I began to think that there was so much which could be leveraged and I said, 'Look, you have done this in four hours' time and I think it is amazing for the time you all got to prepare. But I want to be grounded more in the specifics, so I am giving you 10 days' time to make a presentation with a more comprehensive action plan a workable plan. You can call in similar people in other plants and have a full-fledged discussion about the plan. This plan should be something which everyone should get committed to and can be easily monitored.' I said, 'Look, for these 10 days please focus only on this, you won't be doing your regular job, as this is urgent and needs to be implemented at the earliest.'

~ Empowerment with Accountability—
providing not only a challenge but also resources and support

We were bleeding and speed was of great essence. The sooner we stopped the bleeding the better it was. And here I could see I'm onto a thing that can be actually made into a very workable plan. I could see that this was the moment to strike to move ahead fast.

*~ Excellence in Execution—*a sense of urgency to implement the needed change

After the 10-day period, when the plan was being presented, I had my senior colleagues sit in the presentation and asked them to either accept or critique the plan. But if they accepted, then they had to take the ownership to make it happen. There were no major objections from the senior colleagues to the plan put forth by the team. This was the meeting where I set the target of reducing costs by 10 per cent.

*~ Entrepreneurial Drive—*a very challenging goal

I told my people that 'we will monitor our progress so that we are absolutely clear whether we are really getting the cost reduction or not, and I will personally monitor the progress each month.' We then created a team to make it happen, I was determined to make it happen. Those who are not into it will have to go; although I didn't say this so specifically but it was understood that we have no option but to stop the bleeding. . . . I think they felt that I'm a no nonsense guy and I will not accept if they don't do it consciously and sincerely. They knew that I was very much capable of going into the 'details' myself.

~ more personal *Excellence in Execution* communicated to the team as part of *Driving Change*

They knew that I could get to the depth of things, so they shouldn't give me half-truths or try to bluff around. I told them to put in their best efforts and make it happen at the earliest.

*~ Empowerment with Accountability—*sets criteria for success

When we started reviewing after a period of 2 to 3 months, we found that it was possible to do this. This was the first breakthrough. It was the third

review meeting and the person who was presenting said, 'We didn't realize that this was possible. But today I can see that we can be very close to
it and therefore we must do our best to make it happen.' I thought that
this was one of the biggest breakthroughs. As I said earlier; we were
looking for ways and means to create that team that could see the ray of
light in the darkness. And when this message came from these people, I
knew I had got the first success as self-realization was the biggest factor.
Once they realize things themselves, it becomes much easier as then you
are not pushing them. The person is going more or less on his own, and
it's like you know pressure cookers; first you put it on high heat and then
the pressure builds up, but after that you put it on low heat. Till self-
realization comes, you are putting on high heat and once that happens,
you are putting on low heat. By the end of the year, which was 9 or 10
months from then, we achieved 8.5 per cent cost reduction.

While a turnaround may be the most dynamic challenge a
leader can face, and may require the greatest combination of
competencies, it can also be avoided by timely interventions
in the form of improvements in an existing business or through
the launch of new product/services. These situations—and the
competencies used by Indian CEOs to address the same—are
discussed in the following chapters.

10 In Improving a Business

While turnarounds are dramatic, it is better for the business to change and improve before matters become critical. This requires frequent—if not continuous—efforts to re-align the business model to the changes in the market, the competition, the technology. Nine of the stories in this study focused on improving the capabilities of an existing business that was performing acceptably well, but could do better. The things the leaders did to improve their businesses included:

- Changing the organizational culture (to be more fast-moving, performance-oriented and/or externally focused);
- Re-organizing the enterprise (to be more effective);
- Introducing new and improved technology into the existing business, and expanding their capability;
- Making specific improvements in the business's processes, or quality and design of products; and
- Improving the company's position through marketing or re-branding the products.

Some of the most successful efforts involved a combination of efforts (e.g. a change in marketing strategy, along with a cultural change internally, and re-organization to support the new marketing position). The only specific type of change that appeared to have a greater chance of success was the introduction of new and improved technology.

The outcomes of the five *most effective* stories included clear accounts of sustained change (i.e. significant improvement in market position in two cases; a detailed account of improvements in the people's behavior—to take more responsibility and initiative; and a change in the structure of the enterprise that produced the desired effect; successful adoption of new technology). The four *less effective* outcomes ranged from 'some change in attitudes, but not as much as was desired and needed', to 'it is too soon to tell' to 'the desired changes were not well accepted or implemented'.

Box 10.1: Formula for Success in Improving a Business

Most stories—both more successful and less successful—include innovation:

- *Networking* for ideas pertaining to technology, good business practices, etc. from other companies and, often, from other countries.
- *Adaptive Thinking* to recognize, *modify* and adapt good ideas to suit the specific needs of the organization/business and the Indian market.

For real success (leading to an improved organization, with better performance), include 'Energizing the Team', by:

- *Driving Change*: not only in thoroughly communicating the desired change, but also in building this change into the structure and processes of the organization.
- *Empowerment with Accountability*: delegating authority, providing a context and the limits for action; but supporting the independence and judgment (of the team) within that context.
- *Team Leadership*: helping the team to be more effective and clearer about its focus and direction.

The *less* successful stories displayed more personal drive for business results (*Entrepreneurial Drive* and *Excellence in Execution*) than focus on Energizing the Team.

'Energizing the Team' Characterized the Most Successful Improvements

In order to be truly effective, the CEO of a large organization cannot personally implement and sustain a growth effort; the commitment and efforts of many people in the organization must be directed toward the same end. Therefore, CEOs were most effective in producing lasting improvements or growth when their focus on **Energizing the Team** was strong and when they used a broad range of behaviors to stimulate their people's energy, enthusiasm and ideas. Four of the five most successful instances of improving the organization included all three of the **Energizing the Team** competencies, and the fifth story included high levels of two of the three team competencies. In contrast, none of the less successful stories included all three of the **Energizing the Team** competencies— and half of these stories included only one of the three competencies.[1]

Empowerment with Accountability appeared most consistently in this scenario: *all* of the 'most effective' stories about improving existing businesses included true empowerment (Levels 3 or 4: delegating authority to make decisions and take action, within well-defined context and limits with the support of the CEO). Often the CEO delegated authority for particular decisions to a team or group of experts. As one CEO said:

> The negotiations were done by a sub-committee, along with a leader. Working under the leader is a group of technology experts who suggest technological requirements, which the leader looks into and negotiates for. Their judgement is adhered to; there is no point in finding fault with their decision. They negotiate and we accept, as there is no point in having a committee and then pulling the rug from under their feet. So once you have a committee you give them the power and let them negotiate. Once they negotiate and come back saying 'this is the best that can be done', all right, we accept it. [And the CEO did just that, by defending the committee's decision against external criticism.]
>
> ~ *Empowerment with Accountability*

On other occasions, there was an individual (chief of a plant, in the case below) who was given authority to act.

> After I discussed this idea with the senior management, I created an owner [of the initiative] from among the people who are manufacturing the product. My role was mostly to 'monitor' and support them. In the meeting I said, 'It's the plant "chiefs" who are going to own this... and the service department.' So they went back and worked backwards. They are very diligent people and are very good at all the root cause analysis. Initially we used to check 142 items which, in a year's time, was reduced to 43 items and will become zero in another year.
>
> *~ Empowerment with Accountability*

Valuable as it is, both in terms of improving the current performance and of developing people's capabilities, *empowerment* alone is not enough to ensure a change that is fully successful and sustained. All of the best stories in this group also included *Driving Change* and/or *Team Leadership* (illustrated in the 'Pure for Sure' case study, Chapter 4). The change must be widely communicated to all the relevant groups within the organization and worked into the normal structure and operating processes of the organization. This might involve changes in structure, in communication practices, in compensation, in funding of different functions within the organization. It may even include publicizing the change to the general population, in order to help ensure that the change becomes permanent (*Driving Change*, Level 4). Usually, the leadership team needs to be strengthened and helped so as to be more effective (*Team Leadership*). This strengthening is often focused on the people closer to the CEO and may include training and developing the team members, improving the team's communication process, helping clarify their priorities and the vision for the organization and for them as a team.

Innovation: Searching for Best Practices as well as New Technology

The most consistent pattern in stories on improving or growing an existing business was the search for best practices, good ideas and new technology. This was seen as a combination of *Networki.ıg* (i.e., looking for new ideas outside one's organization) and *Adaptive Thinking* (i.e. understanding the business environment and finding new ways to operate within it). While each story had at least one of these two competencies, most stories included both.

One leader expressed his satisfaction at his ability to both—find new high-technology equipment overseas and then to adapt and transfer that technology for manufacturing in India.

This leader was quick to perceive the need to significantly upgrade the technology supporting the services that his organization was providing to India. He understood that, without this upgrade, the scope of international commerce would be limited in the future. It was especially important to him that this very high-tech equipment be

> ...manufactured in India. That is a strong point because the foreign firms charge too much; so that, if you buy equipment manufactured here, you can contain the base cost...we take the technology (developed elsewhere) master it, make it our own and supply it. There is a satisfaction that it is manufactured in India. True, the technology is American; but the components they buy from the world market are assembled and supplied in India. And then we can supply what we need.... It was part of this is a continuous process of technology upgrading but it was satisfying that you would set a target of installing locally supplied equipment—and meet it.

Although many innovations are technology-related, others are related to business process, quality and customer service. Bold goals can be set—and met—in these areas as well.

Another leader realized that the dealers, who sold his company's products, spent hours inspecting the products before selling and were not too happy about this. He had a 'radical' idea of improving the consistency of the quality of the products—to the extent that dealers would need to spend *no* time inspecting them. This goal, of significantly reducing the necessary inspection time, became the means of organizing a dramatic improvement in the quality of the product—and, thus, in the way the company approached the question of quality.

Improvements are *Less* Likely When 'Socially Responsible Business Excellence' Outweighs 'Energizing the Team'

One of the differences between an entrepreneur, or the owner of a small business, and a CEO is that the former can run well on his/her own drive for business excellence. One of the primary roles of the CEO is to encourage and draw out the entrepreneurial excitement, the focus on execution and the adaptive thinking of *the rest of the people in the organization*. The competencies needed for this are not merely the leader's own *Entrepreneurial Drive* or *Excellence in Execution*. Indeed, the *balance* between **Socially Responsible Business Excellence** and **Energizing the Team** clearly distinguishes the most successful accounts of *improving a business*. In *every* effective case of improving business practices or growing an existing business, the CEO gave *more* attention and skill to **Energizing the Team** than to **Socially Responsible Business Excellence**. In *every* less effective case, there was as much or more focus given to the leader's own thoughts about **Socially Responsible Business Excellence**[2] (this was true even though some individual leaders told one more effective story and another less effective story, both about improving their existing business). **Socially Responsible Business Excellence** competencies are counter-productive in growing a business *if they distract the leader from Driving Change, from Empowering with Accountability or from exercising good Team Leadership*. A little bit of both, *Entrepreneurial Drive* and *Excellence in Execution*, serve well in these scenarios. The trick is to get the balance right. Within each scenario of improving the business, the leader needs to have considerably more focus on **Energizing the Team** than on his personal business orientation. In that sense, **Socially Responsible Business Excellence** needs to be drawn more from others in the organization, than personally from the leader.

Overall, it is the leader's ability to first gather ideas for innovation (*Networking*), and chose a focus for improvement (*Adaptive Thinking*), combined with skill and attention to **Energizing the Team** that is most likely to support lasting improvements in the organization.

Notes

1. Statistically significant difference—calculated on the sum of the highest level seen in each of the **Energizing the Team** competencies— $p < .03$, Mann-Whitney U-test. The range of the total **Energizing the Team** score was 6 to 10 for the most successful stories, and 3 to 6 for the less successful stories.

2. The relative strengths of the two clusters were measured by comparing the sums, *by cluster*, of the highest levels of each competency seen within each story. The two groups of stories are statistically significantly different (Mann-Whitney U-test, $p < 0.02$, $n=9$, comparing, for each story, the difference between the sum of the **Socially Responsible Business Excellence** cluster and the sum of the **Energizing the Team** cluster). We could use such a simple measure of the relative strengths of the two clusters because both clusters had the same number of competencies and the same target levels.

11 In Launching Something New

The third group of stories focused on starting a new product or service, diversifying the line of business, adding new technology or starting a new line of business. Considering our interviewees were leading large and successful organizations, most of their stories were not about starting an entirely new organization but rather about starting a new line of business as a part of the existing enterprise. Most new businesses included some sort of innovation—technological at times, or in terms of products or services being offered. These 'start-ups', though they always have a chance of failing, are the strongest engine of economic growth. Compared to samples of CEOs from other, more 'developed' countries, Indian CEOs told an unusually large number of stories of starting new operations, many being the 'first in India'. These stories included some aspects of improving the organization's capabilities, but with the additional theme (and stress) of introducing significantly new products or services in the market. Leaders often described their situations with phrases such as 'never been done before', 'totally new' or 'a really new kind of . . .'.

Six 'most successful' stories of *launching something new* spoke of operations that were well-established, highly successful and, generally, also well-known to be successful; one story was about an operation that was quite successful—until the market changed again. In six of the seven 'partly success-ful' stories leaders expressed some satisfaction with the results, and spoke of ongoing operations that were not (at the time of the interview) on a solid, profitable and well-established footing. There was also one clear 'failure', no longer operating, that made for a very helpful and instructive example.

Embarking on a new enterprise—or a new venture within an existing one—calls for many of the same characteristics as in the turnaround of an existing business. Along with excitement

---

Box 11.1: Formula for Success in
Launching Something New

Most stories include SCRIBE competencies and Inner Strength:

- *Entrepreneurial Drive* (sometimes with *Excellence in Execut-ion*)
- *Adaptive Thinking* (often supported by *Networking*)
- *Transcending Self* and/or *Executive Maturity* at basic levels

Real successes (established, ongoing business ventures) include:

- The **Energizing the Team** cluster of competencies,[1] including *Team Leadership, Driving Change* and *Empowerment with Accountabil-ity.*
- More **Inner Strength**[2]: Although most stories on launching a new business included *Transcending Self* or *Executive Maturity*, the more successful ones included still higher levels of both these compe-tencies.
- More numerous and sophisticated competencies overall.[3]

There are no counter-productive competencies when it comes to launch-ing something new.

---

[1] A statistically significant difference (p <.01, calculated on the sum of the highest level for each competency in the cluster, n=13).
[2] A statistically significant difference (p <.05, calculated on the sum of the highest level for each competency in the cluster, n=13).
[3] A statistically significant difference (p <.05, calculated on the sum of the highest level for all competencies in the story, n=13).

and hope, there is also a great deal of uncertainty, as the leader must determine which investments to make, when to bring in new employees and how to train them. Often, there are questions pertaining to technology: what technology to use and how to adapt the same to the enterprise's specific needs. In several cases, there was significant organizational change needed to design and produce the new products, and even to find new ways to design and produce new and better products.

Often the start-up effort required obtaining governmental permissions, but the leader talked about the lobbying for these permissions as a separate story, and therefore the efforts to deal with the government are analyzed separately.

Like a turnaround, launching a new business-requires a combination of competencies.

Socially Responsible Business Excellence Supports Innovation in Launching New Products or Services

The business-related competencies of *Entrepreneurial Drive* and *Adaptive Thinking* are expected when launching something new. Obviously essential to the start-up process, these competencies reflect how and why a leader tries to launch a new business in the first place. Most stories about launching a new business included adapting products or technology specifically to Indian conditions and materials (but without sacrificing quality!). Innovation in products or technology was often a key element of the start-up. While at times these stories involved providing needed goods or services to the lower parts of the economic pyramid, at other times they involved creating world-class capabilities in India. Almost always there was an awareness of how this new enterprise would fit and support the larger economic picture of India— a kind of awareness *not* found in business leaders of the West. In a start-up (as compared to improvement in an ongoing business discussed in Chapter 9), the leader's personal engagement—with new ideas and new venture—seems to help and not hurt the business. In this situation, perhaps because of increased business risk, employees need to draw additional confidence and energy from their leaders' enthusiasm and commitment to the new venture. In the case of improving an already established venture, employees have less uncertainty and need to feel the space to contribute their own innovations.

One leader recognized that, with the changes in the Indian market, his company would have to completely change their approach to technology and the design of new products:

What has given me the greatest satisfaction during this period has been my focus on technology development in the company. Technology (in this industry) changes very rapidly; only those companies which can move rapidly with the technology can survive in this kind of a market situation... Then, things started changing with the Indian government's policies of globalization and privatization. The procurement methods of Indian customers as well as parts of the government underwent a rapid change. They started floating tenders... Now when we give our proposal to our own customer, or the government or other government customers, our proposal is evaluated along with the proposal they receive from other international companies. When that kind of competition comes in, the customer evaluates in favour of that proposal which addresses his requirements of technical features and operations capabilities. This is something which I recognized and underlined. I told all my people that the time has come for us to manage our product technology in such a way that when the next customer requirement comes, we have a product that meets the customer requirement almost fully. Today it is not enough to be 'state of the art'; we must have a 'futuristic state of the art'. We must design those products that will meet the customer's needs as they emerge two or three years from now. The first thing was for the company to singly focus on speedy technology transformation.

> ~ *Adaptive Thinking*; additional competencies were used to
> actually launch the new products and new design process

Leaders mostly used *Networking* to gather, test and refine their ideas before implementing them. They were bold in going far afield to get inputs and ideas from business or technical leaders in other countries as well as in India, asking anyone they thought might be able to help. They gathered technical ideas, or business practices, which they then adapted to the Indian conditions. In some instances they also coached subordinates, even very young employees, to build relationships abroad which they could later draw upon for assistance.

Although there was only one account of a clear failure, this was a valuable and illuminating story as the leader was quite frank about what he saw as the source of the problem: he 'did not do anything different' (i.e. he did not use *Adaptive Thinking* in this situation although he did use it in other situations) and he didn't *network* until it was too late. Every other start-up included either *Networking* or *Adaptive Thinking*; most included both.

Inner Strength and Energizing the Team Help Ensure that the Start-up will Take Hold and Grow

The leader's **Socially Responsible Business Excellence** is necessary, but far from sufficient, to launch something new. The whole team of employees must become engaged and committed to making the new venture a success, to helping it take hold and grow. And it is the leader's responsibility to empower and inspire them to do so. The competencies leaders consistently use for this crucial task are:

- The **Energizing the Team** cluster of competencies, including *Team Leadership, Driving Change* and *Empowerment with Accountability*.
- More **Inner Strength** *(Transcending Self* and/or *Executive Maturity)*. Even though most of the launching of

new business stories included some *Transcending Self* or *Executive Maturity*, the more successful stories included still higher levels of these two competencies.

In this scenario, no single behaviour was associated with success (in the way that *Adaptive Thinking* was for the turnaround situation). The difference was, rather, in the amount and variety of **Energizing the Team** competencies, with the most effective instances including both a larger number of these competencies and more sophisticated levels of these competencies, described in Chapter 6. All of the most effective stories included at least two of the three **Energizing the Team** competencies at moderate to high levels of sophistication. *Both Team Leadership* and *Driving Change* appeared in five of the six most effective stories, but none of the less effective stories had both these competencies.

Clearly, the effectiveness of a start-up depends greatly on the leader's ability to engage and energize his/her team to fully execute—and sustain—the venture. Doing so also lends the project the benefit of the team's ideas and energy. This is a multi-stage process, beginning with strategizing and planning the implementation. Then comes communicating the vision and plan—not just once, but over and over again in different ways and to different groups within the enterprise; repeating the importance of the message. Generally, the message, the change or the vision that the leader is communicating and building into the organization is one that is grounded in the **Socially Responsible Business Excellence** competencies. However, in the most successful stories, the leaders' focus is more on communicating and sharing their ideas and their urgency for action, and also on stimulating these qualities in their employees.

Note the *Excellence in Execution* and the *Entrepreneurial Drive* that shape and motivate the change this particular leader is driving:

I should say communication convinced them about the need for this. I remember the times when I used to tell them, 'Unless we do this in the next two to three years, the company will go down.' Then I told the top R&D managers to come up with as many projects as possible, focusing on their own area of activity and then see how the product can be developed later. I said, 'Don't come with just a marginal incremental improvement. Aim at having a substantial improvement in the product specification such that we are able to easily compare with international products as we are going to compete with international companies. And once this message was given to the R&D managers, they came up with a proposal for development—either upgrading existing product or developing new products.

This leader also spent considerable time with teams of engineers, helping them break a seemingly impossible task into its components and sub-components; showing them how they really could accomplish it, and infusing them with confidence and energy.

I explained to them how to proceed with this. 'We should study the best products that are in the world market today but we should not stop there. This is the first benchmark. We should also try to do a technology forecast which would help us know where the product is likely to be three or four years from now. Then our target focus should be linking the projected forecast to the technology level, not the current level, but to what it is likely to be three years or four years from now.' So our engineers are constantly reminded by me and now, of course, by many of my colleagues too, that whenever you take on the development of any new product, this concept of futuristically state of the art had to be retained... I said this to so many people, so many projects; I had to do it in almost every factory.

– this *Driving Change* message also contains *Excellence in Execution*

Just describing the change is not enough—the leader must also follow it through:

The next important thing is monitoring and spending time with them. This is essential as it enables them and ensures that they are completing things fast enough. If an R&D project is going to take five years, it may get outdated by the time it's done; thus it was very important that we realize this in say 15 months/18 months.

– *Excellence in Execution*—a sense of urgency

When I review and monitor they usually say, 'Well it's going to take time' or, 'I have this problem because this particular component is not available or my key engineer who is working on this has left the company.' This is when I step in to find supporting measures for them—either by moving some other engineers who could replace the original or by getting that material from somewhere else. That kind of support just helps them complete the projects on time or nearly on time.

> ~ Team Leadership—ensuring that his own actions were consistent with the message Team Leadership—supporting the team and providing the necessary resources and encouragement, and also Excellence in Execution—taking action

The leader must also make structural changes that will allow the change to endure: resources must be made available, re-allocated; and systems must be aligned to support the new direction.

On the management side, we prepared resources in terms of finance and people, as well as recruitment for this purpose. There was no restriction at all. They just have to tell us what they need; our objective is, 'We want to upgrade every product of the company within the next two years and parallely we want a completely new version of the product to be brought out in two to three years to match with the emerging requirements of the customer.

Several leaders combined Empowerment with Accountability with Transcending Self by insisting that the new operation should be fully managed by Indians, even against the advice of foreign suppliers or consultants who felt that their own expertise would be needed on an ongoing basis. As India's technical and intellectual capabilities are recognized by the business community world wide, this situation is already becoming less common. Nevertheless, the underlying faith in Indian abilities, plus the care that these leaders took to ensure that their employees received the appropriate training and development, is likely to continue to be of significant value, especially in start-up scenarios.

These leaders ensured that their young technical or management teams received the necessary training, and provided them with advice and encouragement to get the most benefit from such opportunities. A leader's faith in the employees' abilities was rewarded by excellent performance. In other cases, *Empowering with Accountability* was shown by appropriately delegating authority to employees or groups of employees—and then supporting them fully.

> [A critical issue for a new business was obtaining the right new equipment at an affordable price. A certain overseas supplier was using his own connections in the Ministry to try to ensure that the more expensive option was accepted. The CEO personally received many calls trying to influence the decision.] Because they [the engineers on the tender committee] were also directly called by the Ministry, they too were under pressure. I told them, 'Do what you feel is right and, as far as the director from the Ministry is concerned, leave it to me to deal with him. Don't be afraid of what they tell you. As long as I'm there, you are safe; you do your job and I am there to protect you.' They happily went back to their research and made the best recommendation. In fact they were very happy with that.
>
> ~ *Empowerment with Accountability*—gives full autonomy with support

> During the board meeting I asked the tender committee to make the presentation. They recommended the choice that was less expensive and technically the best [but not the choice the Ministry had been asking for]. That presentation was interrupted by those two or three people again and again, but I made sure that the presentation was made and completed. It was a very long process, so we decided to meet again next day. Next day, we met after lunch but kept on discussing about the proposals up to 7 pm or so. The people were trying to raise new issues [to get us to accept the politically desirable product], bringing out new papers. But our tender committee—executive directors of engineering and of contracts, and the finance chief—kept on explaining these things over and over again. I told my people, 'Do not worry about these remarks, ignore these rather personal remarks; but if they point out any problems, then you answer.'
>
> ~ here, the CEO is showing *Executive Maturity* and also encouraging it in his subordinates

> 'If you feel personally attacked, then there's a tendency to respond in a manner which may not be very dignified; you have to keep in control to maintain the dignity of the board.' So they listened to me, but many a time they started saying something and I stopped them, 'No, let's just come to the point.'
>
> ~ more *Empowerment with Accountability*

So, next day after 7 pm, we decided to meet again after 9 pm. I told them, 'I am not closing the meeting without coming to a decision.'

~ Excellence in Execution, basic level

'We have to take a decision because my project will get delayed.' Around 2 am in the night I said, 'Now that we have discussed every point, let's vote.' By way of voting, the recommendation of the tender committee was accepted. When we finished, one of my colleagues asked me, 'How could you keep so cool at 3 am?' My response to him was, 'You can't afford not to.'

~ Executive Maturity—self-management

Most leaders showed at least one of the **Inner Strength** competencies. *Transcending Self* often appeared as a motivation for taking the business risks involved, because the new operation would be good for India as well as for the company; it would provide the required goods or services (often to the bottom of the pyramid) or would improve the overall economy and/or self-sufficiency of India.

One CEO explained why he took the risk to travel all over the world finding unusually good 'deals' on high-tech equipment although he did not yet have the permission to use those equipments. He said,

Hopefully in the future, India will become one of the powerhouses of manufacturing when, with some changes in labour and in rules, a world-class infrastructure will be built. That is really the theme I will address tomorrow night in the management school. India can be a powerhouse of a manufacturer. If China can be, we can be too; in fact we have higher level of skills than China has.

Executive Maturity is used to continue—calmly and effectively—through the frustrations that come with the process of building a new business, and also as the basis of respect and compassion that create the foundation of an effective work culture where all the employees can take pride and find respect in their work.

Although most of the start-up stories included some **Inner Strength**, leaders demonstrated noticeably more **Inner**

Strength in the most effective events. In five of the six most effective start-ups, the leader showed either the very highest level of *Transcending Self* or *Executive Maturity*; or *both* competencies at moderate levels.

Starting a new business venture is a real challenge anywhere in the world, requiring *Entrepreneurial Drive* and *Excellence in Execution*. Real and lasting success comes when leaders add skill and time in **Energizing the Team** so that the new business venture is carried forward with the dedication and commitment of many people in the organization. In addition, **Inner Strength** is required to cope with all the challenges and difficulties surrounding new business ventures.

12 | In Boundary Management

Many an Indian CEO spoke about dealing with the government for permits or permission to take certain actions or adjustments in regulations that would allow them to enter certain markets or to compete effectively. Their stories abounded with concerns about handling inquiries from government, politicians and media. Such elaborate stories of this kind of lobbying (for government permissions, to conduct or expand business) simply do not occur in the transcripts from CEOs, or even high-level executives, in most developed countries. In the West, most permits and permissions are routinely arranged at much lower organizational levels, according to more clearly defined rules and standards. Although Western leaders sometimes complain about what they see as excessive bureaucracy and interference, it is a rare and unusual circumstance when a CEO is personally involved in obtaining permits and permissions. There are a few Western stories about dealing with—or responding to—governmental inquiries from executives in the petroleum industry (generally following an oil spill, shortage or other mishap) and, occasionally, from the health care or health insurance industries. Equally rare in the West are instances of CEOs or executives taking a more proactive role—

to make some positive social change (e.g. adjusting tax laws to encourage more recycling)—but this is not a part of routine ordinary business. However, such related stories would together account for only a very tiny fraction of all stories of the CEOs in the West (less than 2 per cent of the stories in the HayGroup database of more than 4,000 Behavioral Event Interviews with executives and CEOs as compared to 20 per cent of the Indian CEO stories). In comparison to CEOs in all the other countries that the HayGroup has studied, CEOs in India—*from both the private and the public sectors*—spend an inordinate amount of time in boundary management, mostly requesting permissions or adjustments in regulations from the government or responding to governmental or media inquiries.

There were 12 such stories from this sample of 29 Indian leaders. This was the only story-type in which clearly unsuccessful attempts were common (there were six—with comments like 'totally unsuccessful', 'complete failure', 'horribly frustrating'. Even when the CEOs were actually successful in boundary management these events were experienced as difficult and frustrating. *Leaders clearly found this process of dealing with the government difficult and unpleasant, procedures that they would have avoided, if possible.* Each of these stories was a necessary part of a start-up, a turnaround or, occasionally, increasing capability in an existing business. These stories were analyzed separately, because in every single case the leaders themselves thought of dealing with the government or 'boundary management' as a separate event.

In addition, there were a few stories from the private sector about leaders trying to influence investors to provide capital for expansion: these stories had a very different focus and tone and were not included in this analysis.

> Public sector CEOs end up spending a lot of time managing the boundary with the Government and the Parliament.
>
> **~Arun Shourie**
> Former Minister for Communication, IT and Disinvestment

This sample of spontaneous stories about their work (participants were only asked for 'times you felt effective' and 'times that were more difficult, frustrating or when you felt ineffective') clearly confirmed the numerous comments from the expert panels that Indian leaders spend much—far too much—of their time in 'boundary management' and in attempting to keep these 'boundary' issues from absorbing the time and attention of the rest of their organization. *This predicament is not limited to public enterprise—private sector CEOs had almost the same proportion of 'boundary management' stories.*

This is an account of how boundary management is practised.

> But we have this challenge: you have to simultaneously tackle frustrations as well as opportunities. You cannot allow your team to feel the difficulty you are facing, because you don't want them to be discouraged. I try to shelter people such that they do not have to worry about things from any event that would distract them. By and large, I think, the organization came to know of this challenge because of the media writing all about this particular issue. Otherwise, internally, I say to them, 'Don't worry about it, you carry on with your work.... There are always shocks and this is a part of it.' Even today, there are other shocks and this would keep on happening. You have regulars or the Parliament or somebody else asking you questions, but, you (the CEO) need to tackle it well and contain the events. Small groups handle it (boundary management) so that the rest of the organization does not know that something is wrong. This is something that I have come to practise in our lives.

Did you think this quote came from a leader of a publicly-held company? *It did not:* this story and many others like it came from India's private sector. We *have not seen anything comparable in the West, be it the CEOs or executives of companies.*

Box 12.1: Formula for Success in Boundary Management

Most stories—both successful and unsuccessful—include Managing the Environment:

- *Stakeholder Influence:* generally supported by *organizational awareness* applied to the government. These competencies were somewhat stronger in the more successful events.[1]

Real success in boundary management depends on Inner Strength:

- *Transcending Self:* to focus one's efforts on what is best for India, and to find the courage to pursue that vision.
- *Executive Maturity:* to persist, and to encourage and sustain others in the face of great difficulties and delays.

Adaptive thinking is *counterproductive*

- All the unsuccessful events included *Adaptive Thinking*: none of the effective ones did.

[1] Statistically significant difference (t-test, $p < 0.05$, n=12, calculated on the sum of the highest levels of the three Boundary Management competencies).

Adaptive Thinking is Counterproductive When Dealing with the Government

In the successful attempts to deal with the government and other outside opinions, the CEOs **did not use** *Adaptive Thinking*. This 'thinking like a business-person' competency appeared in *all* of the unsuccessful boundary management attempts, and *none* of the successful efforts:[1] (*i*) any level of *Adaptive Thinking* (even Level 1) was perfectly associated with *failure* in dealing with the government; (*ii*) *every un*successful boundary management story included *Adaptive Thinking* (considering the impact of the changes on the companies own profitability, talking about desired changes as a business opportunity); (*iii*) *none* of the successful events included *Adaptive Thinking*.

Clearly, thinking like a businessman is *not* the way to get the government to agree with you! The most effective leaders used *Adaptive Thinking* in other situations, but seemed to put it out of their minds in these boundary management situations, focusing instead on what was best for India as a country. This ability to turn a fundamental competency—like the basic way you think about problems on and off, according to the situation—is quite unusual.

Leaders Used Straightforward Influence Methods

In contrast to leaders elsewhere who use the competencies of *Stakeholder Influence* and *Organizational Awareness* for a wide variety of purposes, the bulk of the Indian leaders' use of these competencies occurred in the context of dealing with the government. Perhaps the best Indian CEOs find the process of dealing with the government so difficult that they avoid the competencies they associate with it.

It was striking that—in comparison to the few Western leaders engaging in dealings with their governments—the methods of Indian leaders were straightforward, without a great deal of complexity or sophistication. When less effective, they make a clear and straightforward business case, along the lines of 'allowing us to do this would produce such-and-such benefits'. When more effective, they sometimes make a clear and straightforward case that allowing the venture would benefit India in a particular way. They also pay attention to their audience, showing some understanding of how to address the concerns of a particular Ministry, or using a good sense of timing—when to push and when not to. At best, they have established some credibility and goodwill with one or more Ministries, which helps smoothen the way. What these Indian leaders do *not* do, is use complex, 'political' manoeuvres used by leaders elsewhere (such as building unseen support for a proposal, or making alliances and trading favours, or sophisticated ways of structuring a group discussion to obtain acceptance of an idea by, for example, surfacing objections in a way that allows someone else to minimize the impact of the objections).

We are not sure why this is the case with Indian leaders; it could be the genuineness of their interest in and concern for the development for their country. Then again, it could be their entrepreneurial drive—perhaps they have, all their lives, been so focused on achievement and entrepreneurial growth that they have not developed sophisticated skills to influence others. Or, for that matter, it could simply be that more complex methods of influence would not be well received (they might be perceived as tricky or unfair).

Inner Strength Helps when Dealing with the Government

When CEOs were successful in their efforts towards boundary management, they were more likely to use *Transcending Self* (considering and appealing to the greater good of India) and *Executive Maturity* (empathy for others and embodying the aspirations of the enterprise). In general, the concern for the country that these outstanding leaders showed in their stories of dealing with the government was sincere and genuine. It was consistent with the concerns they expressed in other settings, not always demonstrated as an argument that they made to others but often expressed in response to, 'What was your thinking about that decision?' or 'What was going through your mind at that moment?'. Even when the leader did not say 'Do this to help India be great', the genuineness of the CEO's concern for the development of the country had a significant impact on ministers and others whose influence was needed. Perhaps it had a greater impact than the words and arguments the leaders would have otherwise used.

Dealing with the government was often a complex process that stretched over months or years and drew on many competencies, as illustrated in this leader's case:

[For many years this leader's organization had wanted to grow in a certain way, but] 'What was preventing us?' A regulation was preventing us.... Finally, I said, 'we have to work out something.'... Well, we worked along with the others in the same industry, and showed how our industry was under threat. And it had to survive, so we could each provide economic support to the country.

~ *Transcending Self*—the purpose was the greater good

We prepared a report for one section of the government. We were driving it. Somebody else was chairing it, but two of my colleagues were the actual people who wrote the report.

~ *Stakeholder Influence*

They [the section of the government] got the report, they looked at it, and they said, 'There is merit in it, but the time is not right; and there are other issues.' They accepted the concept. After a little while, we [had] kept the pressure up so, the government said, 'Yes, we may allow it.' So we went back to the proposal. They had no intention of allowing it; they literally threw it out and just shot us down. The media got onto it and said that all of us had dashed through this [project], and that we were not doing it very well. The media was bashing us saying 'No'. They were sending us a clear signal that this is not the [right] time.

Yet, the leader did not give up:

I came back to my team and said, 'We will fight this one out, we will not let this one off.'

~ *Executive Maturity*

We kept plugging at it and we then started building alliances with another Ministry. You can play your card in different ways. You can go to the (most obvious section of the government) or you can go to [a different] Ministry. The other part of the government is not answerable to the Ministry. But you have a structure here where 80 percent of this industry in India is controlled by the first Ministry because they own (the companies). And so the relationship is a bit nebulous, it is not straightforward.

~ *Organizational Awareness*

Then the leader took the lead, within an industry group, to go to the government for changes in the regulation:

...because the earlier report was a joint report and everybody realized that we were running into trouble in terms of raising money. We can only raise money if we can grow (in the way that the regulations prevented). Everybody knew that the difference was that my company was working at this strategy. I had new products. I started developing leadership in those products. I was conducting all those businesses; I created organizational structure, and I created the capital.

~ Excellence in Execution—taking actions to create opportunities

The other companies were exactly as they were earlier, but they knew there was a problem happening. They found it suitable to join the wagon and say, 'Look, we have to change.' I clearly knew that it would not be easy for them to change, because it may not be easy for me but it was not impossible.

~ Organizational Awareness

So we started getting a sympathetic ear from the Ministry. They started asking a whole bunch of questions as to why I was starting this. How did we get that sympathetic ear? Well, for many years (before this), I had frequent contacts with certain people in the Ministry—not as a lobby group. My company was their sounding board on...various government initiatives. If there was work to do, my company would do it. Very simply, I would always say, 'My talent pool is yours. Tell me what needs to be done and I will get it done.' I never influenced them in terms of business. All the things we had done were simply acts of goodness. 'We need to do it for national language? We will do it.'

~ Transcending Self

In that way we were involved in every single Ministry, be it law, sports, etc. We did work for all of them; literally for them. We don't charge anything. I have a four-to-five-men team working on it. So now the Ministry believed that my company had goodwill. The Ministry started asking tough questions and the questions started getting tougher and tougher, and then one of the other companies started running into capital problems. They started going to the government with begging bowl, 'Give us some money.' So I started saying, 'Hey, these people are coming and pressing us for money.'

~ Stakeholder Influence

[Even so there was another round of influence.] Finally, to cut a long story short, we saw the first sign that the Ministry may allow us to [grow the way we wanted] and that's when we made our pitch. They shot us down, maybe September, October...[After more reports and proposals they could] see that the Ministry was clearly changing their character, their mind...I didn't have to push too much. The system pushed; or, rather, the other companies pushed toward disaster. So ... actually the Ministry made the change by then on its own steam. I didn't have to push anymore. [Even after the Ministry changed the regulations, there were such difficult conditions and requirements that] when the requirements came, the analysts saw it and they said it was impossible, no one could possibly make it under these conditions. I said that we would take it in our hands. I look at any of these strategies as a challenge. It is like a mathematical equation. What are the missing links? Can you find an answer to these missing links? If 'yes' [then] in what way. Who needs to work on this, and what is the team effort? If 'no'—you cannot find an answer to missing links—then put this in one or two blocks where we know the answer is impossible, you can't resolve it. (So when he went back to the government, he could say) 'I am not asking for the moon here, just something very logical. All the other things look tough but we can find solutions. Some may say it is impossible but not us, we will find a solution.'

~ *Stakeholder Influence*

First, I look at it strategically, put it in context and then look at it in terms of how we shall do it. Execution. Then it needs the government to make the relaxation start. So I meet the person from the government, tell him the problem, and find out from him how far he is willing to go.

~ *Networking*—to get crucial information

Then we can tell the team, 'This is something you can do, this is something you cannot do. I believe that this is what I can get from the government but nothing more.' (And the government made just enough relaxation of the requirements—'nothing substantive'—to make the growth possible.)

An Unresolved Problem: The Contradictions in the Requirements for Indian CEOs

Table 12.1 summarizes competencies namely, *Added Value*, *Necessary* and *Counterproductive*, in each of the four most frequently seen situations. It illustrates the consistent patterns of competencies according to situations: note that the leaders often needed, and used, additional competencies in response to the specific needs of their unique situations.

Table 12.1: A Summary of Leadership Competencies—Need vis-à-vis Situation

	Turnarounds	Building the Organization	Start-Ups	Boundary Management
SOCIALLY RESPONSIBLE				
BUSINESS EXCELLENCE				
Adaptive Thinking	Highest level is essential for success	In both more and less successful stories	In both more and less successful stories	**Counterproductive if used at all, any level**
Excellence in Execution	In both more and less successful stories		In both more and less successful stories	In both more and less successful stories
Entrepreneurial Drive		**Counterproductive if over-used**		
ENERGIZING THE TEAM				
Team Leadership	In both more and less successful stories	More of these competencies are found in the most successful stories	More of these competencies are found in the most successful stories	
Driving Change				
Empowerment with Accountability				
MANAGING THE ENVIRONMENT				
Networking	In both more and less successful stories	In both more and less successful stories	In both more and less successful stories	In both more and less successful stories
Organizational Awareness				
Stakeholder Influence				
INNER STRENGTH				
Transcending the Self	In both more and less successful stories		Higher levels in the most successful stories*	These competencies are found in the most successful stories
Executive Maturity				

* **Inner Strength** competencies made for the baseline at lower levels, and added value at higher levels in start-up situations.

Table 12.1 highlights an underlying cause of difficulties posed to India Inc.: the contradictory requirements of business leaders. *Adaptive Thinking* (thinking like a businessman) is essential for business growth—whether in a turnaround or in a start-up or in building an organization. However, many of these situations also call for dealings with the government (for permissions, etc.), and in India it is expected that the CEO will be personally involved in these dealings. But any *Adaptive Thinking* leads to failure in dealing with the government (and the media). It is extraordinarily difficult to simultaneously 'think like a businessman' and also *not* 'think like a businessman'. These outstanding leaders have managed to meet such contradictory demands by compartmentalizing, by mentally separating, the two aspects of their work. This is surely why they always spoke about boundary management, dealing with the government, as if it were a separate event altogether. Although these leaders managed this difficult combination of requirements, expecting that most business leaders will be able to simultaneously use and not use the same kind of thinking is not a recipe for success.

Note

1. Statistically significant difference (t-test, $p < 0.01$, n=12, calculated on the highest level observed of *Adaptive Thinking* only).

III

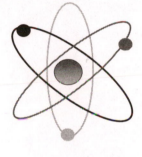

CONCLUSIONS

III

13 Comparisons

'Inner Strength' as a Model for Leaders the World Over

Though there are many similarities among CEOs around the world, as summarized later in this chapter, the Indian leaders stand out as embodying several characteristics that are virtually absent in interviews with CEOs or high level executives elsewhere. These uniquely Indian qualities are all found in the **Inner Strength** cluster:

- The inclusion of considerations of benefits to the larger society *as an intrinsic part of business decisions* (*Transcending Self*).
- Mention of spiritual or religious sources of inner strength. (*Executive Maturity*).
- Demonstration of compassion for the feelings and sufferings of others (*Executive Maturity*).

It is not an accident that these three characteristics appear together. The only places we have seen similar qualities is in outstanding leaders of Catholic health organizations[1] and outstanding leaders of religious orders of nuns and monks.[2] We simply do not find similar statements in the Behavioral Event

Interviews of business leaders elsewhere, notwithstanding how Western leaders may be devout, compassionate and socially aware in their personal lives. The consistent pattern of these themes in BEIs of Indian CEOs is most striking in contrast to their counterparts elsewhere.

Mahatma Gandhi offered the world a practical demonstration of the possibility of combining the best of pacifism (non-violence) with the best of activism (resistance to oppression, efforts to improve society). And, though his example has too often been ignored, the world has been a better place for it.

This group of Indian CEOs offers, quietly, in their everyday business decisions, a practical demonstration of the possibility of combining the best of capitalism (economic growth) with the best of socialism (concern for impact on the society, especially on the poorer members).

Let us discuss this unique Indian ethos of leadership in greater detail, because it seems so unique and also important. First, let us consider what this kind of leadership is *not*.

- It is *not* a matter of fine words and public pronouncements. The evidence we heard came from deep within the stories, often only after several questions along the lines of, 'What were you thinking at that time?', 'Why was that so important?', and 'What was the reasoning behind taking that big risk you just described?' While some leaders gave 'making India great' as the reason for their actions, in other cases this reason may not have been well-known, as the leader seemed to take such thinking for granted, to see it as nothing special. All of us have known leaders who make fine and noble speeches, but whose real decisions are not for the benefit of the country. In contrast, Indian CEOs in our study tended to act more and speak less about the benefits to the country.

- It is *not* a matter of 'assuming' or 'masking the assumption' that your profits are good for the country. This is *not* an Indian version of, 'If it is good for General Motors, then it is good for America.' Indeed, *Transcending Self* is just the opposite; something like, 'If it will be good for India, then of course we will make extra efforts and take extra risks to make it happen.'

- It is *not* nationalism. Although these CEOs—who run some of the largest and most successful businesses in India— think in terms of making 'India' better, the thought pattern is essentially similar to that of small entrepreneurs trained by David McClelland 50 years ago (who thought about making more jobs and a better life for their villages). Only now they are thinking on a larger scale. We did *not* hear any of the nationalist themes of 'my country beating other countries'. This is *not at all* about enriching India at the expense of other countries. Instead, we heard a desire to learn from other countries, to cooperate, to make partnerships, to be inspired by them ('If they can do it, so can we'). Nor did we hear even the slightest hint of the nationalist fervour of 'my country, right or wrong'. Instead, we heard honest appraisals of India's strengths and her difficulties and shortcomings—and a stout willingness to work hard to make things better. We can well imagine that, in another generation, with more global business reach, this same social concern and goodwill may well extend beyond India's borders.

- It is *not* a matter of making enormous profits and then spending them in philanthropy. Though some leaders did make an effort to 'give something back' to the country, and the sponsorship of this research by Bharat Petroleum is indeed an example, such philanthropy, admirable though it is, is not the heart of *Transcending Self*. At most, philanthropy is one very small aspect of *Transcending Self*.

So, What is this Special Leadership?

Transcending Self is about bringing considerations of the benefit to the country into the very heart of the business decision-making process: making *business decisions* that turn on how valuable the outcome will be to the growth and greatness of the country. And, in the stories that we heard, many of these decisions benefited primarily those at the lower part of the economic pyramid. These leaders put their creativity, their *Adaptive Thinking*, their formidable business skills and the resources and energies of their companies to work on projects that would have a positive economic impact on the country as a whole, and especially on the lives of farmers, or of people who want to own their homes, or who really need access to pure and reliable petroleum, or watches, or vehicles, at a reasonable cost. It is about bringing social values, and consideration for the impact on all the stakeholders (not just the shareholders) into the process of making business decisions, about giving these factors serious weight in business decisions. In doing so, these outstanding Indian CEOs drew upon all their personal resources, their values, their compassion for the plight of others and their spiritual practices (from different religions).

Indian CEOs set an example that business leaders in other parts of the world would do well to ponder.

Overall Comparison: The Stories they Chose to Tell...

The experiences of Indian corporate leaders in the overall study hold several pointers to differences with their Western counterparts. The simplest way to compare the two groups of leaders is to look at the main themes in the stories each group of leaders had to tell. The leaders' choice of stories is, in itself, an interesting measure of the similarities and differences between them, because the interviewers were discreet enough not to influence their choice of topics.

While business leaders in the West busy themselves with many issues, in cluding reputation, management, cultural change and succession planning, CEOs of India's top companies have shown tendencies to put all their energies into driving innovation, growth and business results. Compared to their peers in other countries, they showed virtually no focus on internal organizational politics or personnel issues. This is in stark contrast to their Western cousins, who spend less effort on growing their businesses and virtually none on 'boundary management' as it is understood in India—except in the rare cases of scandals or very specific and quite unusual crisis situations, such as major product failures or financial misreporting. Instead, they are more occupied with a host of other issues that the Indian CEOs mentioned rarely or not at all, including:

- Composing and managing their team of direct reports and soliciting inputs from them;
- Internal changes not clearly and directly related to growth (changes in organizational culture, or re-organizations and structural changes);
- Relations with key customers or groups of customers;
- Developing the skills and abilities of their subordinates, preparing potential successors;
- Mergers and Acquisitions and Joint Ventures—both negotiating these contractual relationships and dealing with the integration of the companies afterward;
- Other external relations including Wall Street analysts, industry organizations, possible strategic alliances and concern with competitors;
- Enhancing the prestige and general presence of the company in the wider world;
- Recently (too recently to be fairly represented in our data), CEOs in the US have focused on issues of governance and relationships with their board of directors.

In comparing Indian CEOs to their Western counterparts, it is important to recognize that the former work in a business environment that is different from the latter's, and that these differences surely have a significant impact on the competencies they display and those that are effective. India today, and recently, has been in a period of enormous economic growth and these leaders have been at the forefront of that growth, which may well account for the difference in focus. As India's economy grows and her industries mature, we shall know whether her business leaders' focus on growth is an enduring national characteristic or if it is the temporary result of the current stage of development.

On the other hand, the Indian CEO's current focus on dealing with the government as the major form of boundary management would surely disappear as soon as government's relations with business were simplified and clarified. There was plenty of evidence, within the BEIs, to convince us that this task is one the leaders disliked and would avoid if at all possible.

Competency Comparison: The Indian CEO Competencies and Competencies Found in the Study on the International CEO

In 1994, the HayGroup undertook an international study of the characteristics of outstanding CEOs. This previous study, based on Behavioral Event Interviews just like those conducted for the present project, looked for both the competencies shared by most outstanding CEOs worldwide and the approaches that differed by region. While our earlier study included 28 CEOs—leaders who were well-known and admired in their respective country—chosen from 15 countries, by HayGroup consultants in each country, it did not include Indian CEOs because, at that time, HayGroup did not have an office in

India and therefore did not, at that time, have local consultants to nominate and interview CEOs. We did include South American and Asian CEOs as well as CEOs from North America and many European countries. The full text of the International CEO study is included in the Appendix. Table 13.1 summarizes the similarities and differences in the competencies of the studies on the International CEO and the Indian CEO.

Many of the competencies found in the international study and the present study described similar characteristics and behaviors: these are simply referred to as 'comparable'.

Table 13.1: Summary of Similarities and Differences in Competencies of both the International CEO and the Indian CEO Study

Indian CEOs' Competencies	International Study of CEOs' Competencies	Comments and Comparisons
Socially Responsible Business Excellence Cluster		
Adaptive Thinking	Conceptual Thinking, Analytical Thinking and Decisive Insight	Adaptive thinking has a unique focus on innovation and on the lower half of the economic pyramid.
		Indian CEOs, as a group have a much clearer, more consistent, focused pattern of thinking than did the international group.
Entrepreneurial Drive	Need to Achieve	Comparable
Excellence in Action	Initiating Action	Comparable
Energizing the Team Cluster		
Team Leadership	Leadership	Comparable
Driving Change	Participative Leadership Centralized Authority	These are three different approaches to achieve similar effects. Indian leaders have a consistent approach to implementing change, including building it into the structure and systems of the business. They do not consistently use either the

Table 13.1 contd.

Table 13.1 contd.

Indian CEOs' Competencies	International Study of CEOs' Competencies	Comments and Comparisons
		Participative Leadership style or the Centralized Authority style of leadership.
Empowerment with Accountability	Holding People Accountable is a 'baseline' competency, not featured in the model	There is no international equivalent to the empowering aspect of the Indian competency. This Indian CEO competency very roughly relates to the Participatory Leadership style, but is much more individually focused and, at the higher levels, involves considerably more risk. Holding People Accountable is a rough equivalent of the accountability aspect of *Empowerment with Accountability*, but completely lacks the aspect of empowerment.
This competency is rarely seen among the Indian CEOs we studied, and there is no equivalent in the Indian CEO model	Good Judgment of People	International leaders frequently discuss the reasons for their decisions about individual subordinates; Indian leaders did not. This competency was not seen much in the Indian group, but was quite common and important in the International Study and appears consistently in CEOs and executives in many countries.

Managing the Environment

Networking	Broad Scanning	The international Broad Scanning is much broader, maintaining a wide-ranging awareness and includes media and print sources, while the Indian Networking is focused on obtaining immediately useful

Table 13.1 contd.

Table 13.1 contd.

Indian CEOs' Competencies	International Study of CEOs' Competencies	Comments and Comparisons
		information, usually from other individuals. Indian CEOs add a bold and extensive use of personal contacts that relates, loosely, to the Personal Relationships style of building Business Relationships—but with much less description of building up the relationship and much bolder requests for information.
Organizational Awareness	Organizational Know-how	International CEOs are more attuned to 'politics' within the enterprise, and sometimes externally. Indians have to use more external political influence, but are less likely to apply these competencies internally.
Stakeholder Influence	Impact and Influence	Comparable behaviours, used more frequently in the international sample, and in a broader range of circumstances. International CEOs are more likely to use influence within their companies, and to use more complex strategies.
Inner Strength		
Transcending Self	Social Responsibility	Transcending Self is stronger and more focused in Indian CEOs. Social Responsibility tends to focus more on fairness within the company, involves less personal risk, and lacks the national focus of *Transcending Self*.
Executive Maturity	No real equivalent	

The Public Sector and the Private Sector: Similar or Different?

> The public sector is by and large under the supervision of the bureaucracy.
>
> They have succeeded in instituting 'bureaucratic accountability' which is in the form of being answerable to the CVC, CAG and various other committees, and the parent Ministry itself. However, there is no 'share holder' accountability.
>
> Businesses need adventurism, need people who can take risks, are willing to do trial-and-error and arrive at solutions. This set of capabilities seems to be completely lacking in the very structure in which the public sector is designed.
>
> *There is very little scope to make these things happen unless there is a radical change. Accountability should be the most important element.*
>
> ~ **Arun Jaitley**
> Former Minister for Law, Justice and Commerce

Experts and CEOs, both in our panels and at other venues, speak eloquently about the special role and the special challenges facing the public sector CEOs. They were so insistent about the differences between the sectors (public and private) that we anticipated having to create two different models with a bit of an overlap. That did not happen. Although the public sector CEOs have a special mission and do face special challenges, we were surprised to find relatively few real differences in the competencies demonstrated by leaders in both sectors, or in the types of stories they told. The first hint—that differences between the two sectors were not as great as anticipated—came *when we looked at the generic competency code and saw that there were no significant differences between these two groups.*

When we look at the Indian CEOs' own, customized competencies (described in detail in this book and depicted in Figure 13.1), there are few differences, and only two that are of statistical significance. Although CEOs in the public sector are statistically more likely to show *Empowerment with Accountability* and *Transcending Self*, compared to the private sector, both Indian groups demonstrated this competency dramatically more often than CEOs in other countries, who almost never talk about making their countries strong, let alone making decisions on this basis. This unique focus may be an enduring Indian characteristic—or it may be a function of this particular stage in India's economic development. However, in our interviews with business leaders in other rapidly developing countries we did not come across anything like *Transcending Self* in their business leaders. Only time will tell if this is an enduring trait of Indian leaders.

Meanwhile, we think it serves India well that her best business leaders take the collective good into account when making business decisions. The remaining differences are not statistically significant. CEOs in the public sector demonstrate somewhat higher levels of *Stakeholder Influence* (boundary management), and *Team Leadership*. Private sector CEOs, not surprisingly, demonstrate somewhat higher levels of *Adaptive Thinking* and *Entrepreneurial Drive*, and tend to *Drive Change* and *Network* somewhat more aggressively than their public sector peers. However, all these differences are so insignificant that, with a fresh set of interviews, they might even disappear.

Interpretations and Comments from Experts, regarding the Public and Private Sector Findings

These findings regarding public sector and private sector leaders were discussed with many CEOs and other experts, both in focus panels and privately. The following responses to these findings were frequently heard.

- **Boundary Management**
  All the experts agreed that CEOs in the public sector spend a huge amount of time in managing the interest and involvement of their main stakeholders and of various other agencies. Private sector CEOs, at the same

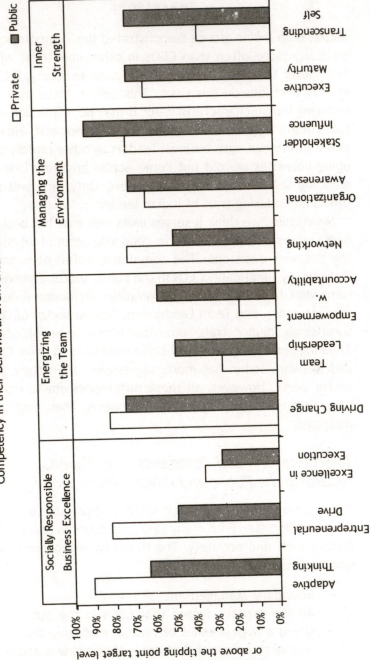

Figure 13.1: The Percentage of CEOs from Private and Public sectors who Demonstrated each Competency in their *Behavioral Event Interviews*

time, are perceived to be clearer in their patterns of governance and their structure.

- **Lobbying with the Government**
  In both sectors, the level of lobbying done by the CEOs is immensely high. The difference being that, while the public sector lobbies with the government for permissions, the private sector does so for licenses. Both groups told stories about lobbying with the government with similar frequency and the same frustration.

- **Empowerment**
  The issue of empowerment also varies with the sector. In the public sector, the CEOs themselves are less empowered, but as they internally empower the people in their organization, they may have more freedom to act within the organization. Whereas, in the private sector, there is lower autonomy as the power is more centralized (and there is a lesser degree of the *Empowerment with Accountability* competency).

- **Networking**
  Unlike CEOs in the public sector, who focus on *Networking* mostly when they run into problems, private sector CEOs maintained their links and networks throughout, owing to their high entrepreneurial drive.

Coming back to the question we began this section with—'the public sector and the private sector: similar or different?'—it is now evident that the two are more similar than we had expected.

> All public sector CEOs are presiding over people's money. We must recognize that we are answerable. The Parliament, the Central Vigilance Commission, CAG are essential since it is public property. The public sector is to make profits but it has a social role which is equally important. Therefore, the role played by CAG, Central Vigilance Commission or the Parliament should not be looked upon as interference in the working of the organization, but must be taken as an occupational hazard.
>
> **~ Ram Naik**
> Former Minister for Petroleum and Natural Gas

Notes

1. 'Transformational Leadership for the Healing Ministry: Competencies for the Future', published by the Catholic Health Association. St. Louis, MO. 1994. On page 31, the 18 competencies for CHA leaders were compared to the competencies in the models of 5 other comparably sized executive roles. The competencies of 'Finding Meaning', 'Faith in God', 'Service to the Poor' and 'Moral Wisdom' were absent from all of the other 5 executive models.

2. David Nygren and Miriam Ukeritis, *The Future of Religious Orders in the United States*. Westport, Conn: Praeger, 1993.

14 The Way Forward

It was 22 January 2005 that brought outstanding CEOs, senior management team members and bureaucrats together to launch the findings of this study. The findings of the study were unveiled by the Indian Prime Minister, Dr. Manmohan Singh. The Deputy Chairman of the Planning Commission, Dr. Montek Singh Ahluwalia, chaired the plenary session while Dr. P.K Basu chaired the session wherein breakout groups deliberated on the findings. The closing session was chaired by P. Chidambaram, the Finance Minister of India. What attracted the who's who of Indian industry and government under one roof was the fact that the summit was unveiling the first ever study of leadership capabilities and competencies of the CEOs drawn from India's best performing and best run companies in the public and private sectors.

The national spirit emerged in all the Indians present. All those who were gathered there called for a movement to turbocharge India's growth. The event led to the emergence of the voice of the people—the voice of the movers and shakers in the economy—who realized that a radical change was needed if India were to leapfrog.

At the CEO Summit, where this study was launched, the participants were divided into three groups and each of these groups had in-depth discussions. These discussions and dis-courses revolved around the ways in which CEOs deal with the numerous constraints that limit the success of their orga-nizations. From the panel discussions that ensued as well as subsequent explorations, the experts made some broad sug-gestions to support India on her road to increased economic success.

Although a great deal of discussion centred on how the government can continue to improve the environment for business and how it can move this change forward even more, there are also roles to be played by an Institute for Advanced Leadership, by the CEOs and their companies, by the media and by education. Let us first address the role of the government.

The Role of Government

The government's reforms programme since the early 1990s has done much to encourage and enable the amazing growth of the Indian economy and of Indian business capabilities.

However, like a referee of the cricket match who is also playing a part in the match, the Indian government is both regulator and investor, and oversees the practical manage-ment of some industries. This double role may have been nec-essary earlier. But now, as the capabilities and resources of the Indian business leaders are approaching and reaching world-class status, the dual role of the government is becom-ing outdated. When the government is also the owner of en-terprises, it needs to figure out how to play its role as owner separately from its role as regulator. Singapore, Malaysia, France and Canada have been suggested as models of situa-tions where the government may own certain businesses but where autonomy in the ordinary, practical operations is given to those public sector enterprises.

The Government as Regulator and Enforcer of Regulations

A big help to enterprise and to foreign direct investment would be the rationalizing of the relationship between the government and businesses, whether public or private, so that 'boundary management' could become a much smaller part and more routine aspect of doing business. As long as the main competitors for Indian businesses were other Indian businesses, the time and energy consumed in 'boundary management' may not have been an efficient use of resources, but it affected all more or less equally. Now, as Indian businesses are increasingly competing, both at home and abroad, with companies from other countries, the effort their leaders expend in managing the boundaries is time and attention the Indian companies can ill afford. The entire relationship between businesses and the *government as regulator* needs to become more transparent, more predictable, less uncertain and less time-consuming.[1] In addition to handicapping Indian enterprises in global competition, the uncertainties, the evident opaqueness and unpredictability of the regulatory processes may also discourage foreign capital investment. Major improvements in the business environment have been made but still more needs to be done in terms of rationalizing and simplifying the enforcement of regulations. Businesses can deal routinely with a wide range of regulations if the process of enforcement is transparent, timely, consistent and predictable.

The Government as Investor/Owner and the Empowerment of the Public Sector

Government is actively involved in business here, while in most countries governments are more at arms length, unless or until some scandalous problems occur. It was repeatedly suggested, by the launch participants, that the Indian government take a more distanced role from businesses, particularly in regard to the public sector enterprises (PSE). It was suggested that public sector boards should be insulated from government interference in their day-to-day affairs. Instead of assuming a position of interference and control, the government should be 'just another stakeholder' for the PSE, possessing the right to enquire and provide support when required. To establish an effective accountability measure, the PSE should have a clearly laid out process of reporting and reviewing performance and a limited number of occasions on which to do this. The debate on this is currently on and various committees appointed by the government are coming up with recommendations to improve the working environment for not just PSEs, but also for the private sector. This work needs to be taken to its logical conclusion.

Although the best PSE CMDs excel at empowering their people, they themselves are currently largely dis-empowered by the government. The empowerment of public sector enterprises could be accomplished by creating an independent board or asset management company, as is seen in Malaysia, Singapore or France, to manage public investments and to allow PSEs to operate more like private sector organizations, with accountable and professional boards of directors. In this context, public sector companies should have to compete and not be protected monopolies. An even playing field for the public and private sector would likely include the public sector no longer seeking protection of tenure of service and also having a significant portion of their compensation related to the performance of the enterprise. Currently, the social obligation of industry to develop the country is largely cast on the public sector. These responsibilities need to be shared by the private sector to further level the playing field for competition. The truly outstanding private enterprise CEOs in this sample tended to take on this responsibility of their own free will. We hope they will continue to do so, and we have seen some additional recent examples of this. In addition, policy frameworks could encourage and support others to do the same.

The Government as Stakeholder

In its role as representing the interests of society as a whole, the government can encourage and support companies to continue to expand the range of products and services offered to the bottom half of the economic pyramid. Bringing the vast under-served population fully into the economic life of the country will promote both economic development and social justice.

Advanced Leadership Institute

Public-private collaboration is needed to set up a centre that will take this work forward by supporting companies in strengthening the leadership pipeline. The focus of such an institute would be on providing senior business leaders with feedback on leadership behaviors and on providing a place to practice and develop them. Such an institute could be a place where executives could meet and share best practices, and where companies could learn from one another as well as from research. An Advanced Leadership Institute would focus on changing leadership behaviors in a practical and visceral way. This would build on the functional content, and on the theories and principles provided by the IIMs and IITs, but would carry the learning into personal and behavioral change. Models for this type of adult learning are found in David McClelland's work in India[2] and in his work on a theory of motive acquisition.[3] Futher elaboration of these methods is found in work funded by the Fetzer Institute.[4] An account of how these principles can be applied in an MBA program is provided by Boyatzis.[5]

In addition, the Advanced Leadership Institute should, in the process of working with CEOs and senior executives, engage in continued research, updating and expanding the leadership competencies as the situation of Indian CEO changes in response to, for instance, the challenges of globalization[6] or the integration of companies acquired in other countries or the increasing demand for talented young Indian leaders. We look forward to seeing the new competencies Indian leaders will find and use in addressing new opportunities and challenges as they arise.

Private Enterprise Boards of Directors and Public Enterprise Selection Board

Those who are responsible for selecting CEOs/CMDs and senior executives can look for these competencies in their candidates (and especially the competencies most relevant to the company's current situation). Boards and others who select executives and CEOs can give CEOs and other executives on-boarding advice and support[7] to enhance the likelihood of success in the new role. At the same time, Indian boards can understand that the CEO, while important, is only a part of the success of the enterprise: the talents and energies of many people working together in an organized fashion are what lead to enterprise success. In this way Indian boards can avoid the mistakes common in the United States: over-emphasizing and over-compensating executives.[8] As the Indian business situation changes and develops, we hope that selection boards will be able to access the resources and ongoing research of an Advanced Leadership Institute to ensure that the pipeline of leaders is full and rich, and to update their understanding of the necessary competencies and qualifications.

Current CEOs and CMDs

Enterprise leaders can use this research now, themselves, in a variety of ways.

- They can remind themselves to place more emphasis on *Energizing their Teams* and not only on business excellence, knowing that Energizing their Teams will help their organizations to implement effectively.[9] The key point is the effective and repeated communication of their vision, so that others can understand it, share it and move forward to implement it. The CEO, especially in larger organizations, must understand that the role of the CEO is *to create the conditions in which others can perform at their best.*[10] They need to create transparency in communications, and thus employee engagement. This can also help them avoid the mistakes of some arrogant American CEOs who seem to believe that the entire success of the company rests on their own personal efforts.

- They can encourage and support each other in ensuring that their business excellence remains socially responsible, that they commit to and maintain codes of ethics and keep the best interests of the nation at heart. (The respect of a close group of peers can be a powerful incentive in these areas, as well as providing a forum where CEOs can think through these issues.)

- They can begin to acquire the talent of listening well to their people, of attending to the individual differences that will enable them to employ their talented people most effectively, to improve their organization's implementation. This practice will also start to prepare them for more complex personal negotiations with potential international partners or counterparts.[11]

- Some participants suggested that CEOs need to think boldly and globally. We felt that the CEOs in the study certainly did that, particularly in the competencies of *Adaptive Thinking* and of *Networking*, but this may be good advice for leaders of new and smaller enterprises.

Enterprises

CEOs and their organizations (including, but not limited to Human Resources)[12] can use this research to move their organizations forward.

- They can start to develop these competencies among their people, encouraging both individuals and the whole system to build up a pipeline of well-prepared leaders for the future, with emphasis on the competencies most relevant to their situation and strategy. This means more than sharing ideas and theories—it means ensuring that people have the opportunity to try out the leadership behaviors on a small scale in their own work, and that they receive encouraging feedback and support when they do so (recognizing that people will initially not be skilled, but that skill and strength are built up through practice with feedback and encouragement). Along with giving feedback on performance results, CEOs and organizations can give feedback on leadership competencies—how well leaders are, for example, empowering their people, or driving change, or conducting their work in an ethical and responsible manner that benefits the larger society.[13] This will help ensure that there are well-prepared candidates available for succession and strengthening the company's ability to implement strategy.
- They can set up the systems and processes that will focus on empowering people in their organization (more *Empowerment with Accountability*, even on a systematic basis). These systems and processes might include means for taking and acknowledging suggestions from front-line employees (i.e., close to the customer, close to the market).
- They can set the conditions, in their organization, for collaboration, teamwork and connecting well with

others (in the service of implementing the necessary direction or change), rather than allowing the organization to focus solely on individual accomplishments. This will have two benefits: (*i*) providing the opportunity for their teams to develop the competencies of **Energizing the Team** and of *Stakeholder Influence* by exercising them within their own parts of the company, and (*ii*) (after people become accustomed to this method of working) allowing more effective implementation as the whole (the team output) becomes, through collaboration, greater than the sum of the parts.

- In some cases the enterprises may need also to invest in basic or technical training to update or expand the skills of the employees in order to help them to become fully productive under changing circumstances. This type of training was provided in some of the stories narrated by the participants of this study. Providing the training needed for productivity demonstrates respect for the employee's innate abilities and helps to evoke self-respect and responsibility.

- It was also suggested that the companies continue to invest wisely in technology, infrastructure and quality so as to compete on an equal basis with other countries.

Business and Popular Media

The media could contribute to moving India's business leadership development forward by presenting role models of Indian leaders in a balanced way—neither over-celebrating nor over-criticizing, but presenting a balanced scorecard in their business reporting. Also, focusing more on the broader teams and how they worked together to accomplish results would encourage leaders at all levels of the organization and avoid the Western mistake of idolizing some CEOs as if they were rock superstars. The media can play a crucial role in helping socialize role models of responsible leadership, especially if it can present models of CEOs who personify the kinds of positive leadership portrayed in this book. It would be of special value to provide role models of leaders energizing their teams or empowering their employees. Examples of positive cooperation among companies could also be helpful in focusing the aspirations of Indian leaders of the future. The media can develop the mindset to celebrate change, celebrate effective implementation and harness change for the advantage of India's prosperity.

Schools and the Educational System

As is often observed by the Prime Minister, the foundation of modern business growth is the education of the population. The quality of primary education must be maintained and made universal. Without literacy and numeracy, it is difficult if not impossible to participate in and actively support the growth of the Indian economy—and today even the small farmers find they can work better with Internet access. At the very least, every child must have sound elementary education. A balanced and wholistic education of the child—with a nurturing focus on developing both emotional intelligence and academic excellence—will help ensure that the leadership pipeline is full for the next generation.[14] Pedagogical methods, for instance, that include team-based learning can help children to develop the ability to work effectively together.

Amazing Growth so far: Great Opportunities for the Future

We all are witnessing the world's largest and most diverse democracy transforming itself and its relationship to the larger world, and also attaining a truly amazing rate of growth and of change. Even since these interviews were collected, much progress has been made in the environment for business, in the Indian infrastructure, and in the rapid expansion and globalization of Indian businesses. This rapid growth has caught the attention and imagination of the Western as well as Indian media. We see much in this study that Western business leaders could benefit by learning from the excellent example of India, as well as a few things that might benefit Indian leaders to learn as they expand their field of operations.

The opportunities for Indian businesses and for the growth of the Indian economy are virtually unlimited, if all the participants in the miracle of growth play their part with the spirit of *Transcending Self*, keeping the needs and the potential of all parts of India in mind.

Notes

1. In addition to our panelists and observers, this suggestion was expounded by C.K. Prahalad (2005) in *The Fortune at the Bottom of the Pyramid: Eradicating Poverty through Profits*. Wharton School Publishing, Upper Saddle River, New Jersey.
2. David C. McClelland, David G. Winter, Sarah Winter, Elliot Danzig, Manohar Nadkarni, Aziz Pabaney and Udai Pareek (1979), *Motivating Economic Achievement*, Free Press, New York.
3. David C. McClelland (1965), 'Toward a theory of motive aquisition', *American Psychologist*, 20 May 1965. See also 'Achievement motivation can be developed'. *Harvard Business Review*, November–December (1965).
4. C. Cherniss and M. Adler (2000), 'Promoting emotional intelligence in organizations: Make training in emotional intelligence effective'. American Society of Training and Development, Washington D.C.
5. Richard Boytazis, Scott S. Cowen and David A. Kolb (1994), *Innovation in Professional Education*, Jossey-Bass, San Francisco.
6. For a useful perspective on globalization, and the appropriate caution in moving toward globalization, see Pankaj Ghemawat, 'Distance Still Matters: The Hard Reality of Global Expansion', *Harvard Business Review*, September 2001, and 'Regional Strategies for Global Leadership', *Harvard Business Review*, December 2005.

7. For research detailing how both selecting for competencies and providing on-boarding advice improved performance in a large multinational company, see David C. McClelland (1998), 'Identifying
Competencies with Behavioral Event Interviews', *Psychological
Science*, 9(5), pp. 331–39. See also, Michael E. Porter, Jay W. Lorsch
and Nitan Nohria (2004), 'Seven Surprises for New CEOs', *Harvard
Business Review*, October.

8. Rakesh Khurana (2002), 'The Curse of the Superstar CEO', *Harvard
Business Review*, September. See also Jim Collins (2001), *Good to
Great*, Harper Business, New York, which suggests that the 'superstar' CEOs are more often associated with a short-term, but not
sustainable, growth while the CEOs who actually produced sustained
growth in the value of their companies were more quiet and modest, and more focused on the accomplishments of the group (what
he calls 'Level 5 leadership', which is in many ways similar to what
we saw in the best Indian CEOs).

9. For example, see R. Boyatzis and A. McKee (2005), *Resonant Lead-
ership: Renewing Yourself and Connecting With Others Through
Mindfulness, Hope, and Compassion*, Harvard Business School Press,
Boston MA.

10. For more details on how to create such conditions for an effective
team see J. Richard Hackman's (2002), book, *Leading Teams: Creating the Conditions for Team Success*, Harvard Business School Press,
Boston, MA. In addition, Richard Hackman, et al, have a new book
forthcoming in 2007 (also from Harvard Business School Press) specifically about effective top teams (CEOs or Business Unit heads and
their direct reports).

11. See *Social Intelligence* by Daniel Goleman (2006), *Social Intelligence:
The New Science of Social Relationships*, Bantam Books, New York.
For a discussion of this area for development.

12. Our experience indicates that these sorts of initiatives are most
effective when HR serves as an advisory and guiding resource but
that the ultimate accountability and 'ownership' of the development efforts belongs to the line leaders, and ultimately to the CEO.

13. For examination of cautionary tale of how an industry failed to do
this, see Paul R. Lawrence (1978), 'Why Do Companies Succumb to
Price Fixing?', *Harvard Business Review*, July.

14. For an in-depth discussion of the role of elementary and secondary
education in competency development, see J. Raven (1984), *Competence in Modern Society: Its Identification, Development and
Release*, Oxford Psychologists Press, Oxford, England.

Appendix
International CEO Study

With international competition intensifying, the most prominent questions, which are troubling almost all executives, are: 'How do I master global leadership?', 'How do you lead an international business successfully?', 'What are superior CEOs doing differently from their average counterparts?', and/or 'How can you ensure that future executives will have what it takes to excel in international organizations?'

Take the instance of a CEO who, during the past 25 years, has overseen an international consumer goods company that is headquartered in Europe. He recalls:

> Our international expansion really developed in two phases. First we spent about ten years restructuring. We wanted to have decentralized operating units managed by a relatively small corporate office. We created a system for regular strategy and planning meetings between our management committee and each of our 17 operational units around the world. This system gives our subsidiaries room to operate in their specific country to area.

By the 1980s, however, the corroboration entered a second phase of international expansion that moved beyond restructuring. According to the CEO, it was a period of 'Intense adaptation' that continues to this day.

> It has become impossible for me—or for any one individual to know everything that needs to be known about all the changes in market conditions, products, manufacturing, and distribution for each country or region. So in the final analysis, you have to find the right people for the right problems—and then trust them to take the right action.

To help them answer this question, Hay/McBer consultants in 15 countries interviewed 55 CEOs, from top-performing corporations across a broad spectrum of industries. The purpose of this cross-cultural study was to clarify the outstanding characteristics of superior CEOs, worldwide.

HayGroup used a scientific approach for identifying competencies called the 'Behavioral Event Interviews'. All the CEOs interviewed were selected because of their outstanding performance in their own country. The criteria used for the selection process included financial performance, market share, stock price measure, analyst ratings and reputations with peers. The sample size for this study worked in a broad range of industries, including manufacturing financial services, oil and gas, retail, consumer goods, information technology, entertainment and communications.

At the same time, researchers selected a sample of 150 high-level executives, across multiple industries from Hay/McBer international database that served as a comparison group. It allowed researchers to identify those characteristics that distinguished superior performance from typical performance.

Our study found no simple recipes. There are many variations in how multinational executives, lead; these differences go beyond the much-discussed issue of diversity in local manners and customs.

Coping with Change: The Two Dimensions of Leadership

The International CEO Competency Study concluded that, to master global leadership, multinational executives must develop two dimensions of leadership:

1. International adaptability
2. Universal competencies

International Adaptability

International Adaptability is the ability to make deliberate choices about conducting business in given area of the world. For example, the study found that:

- *Successful CEOs, operating in the Far East tend to conduct business through* the gradual development of mutual respect and trust. In contrast, superior CEOs in North America may

subordinate personal relationships to more explicit contractual goals.
- The best European CEOs prefer to emphasize the reason and logic of their plan, while their North American counterparts tend to stress the importance of immediate implementation.

A key role for multinational executives, therefore, is to understand the cultural assumptions for doing business in a given part of the world. Hay/McBer hypothesized that multinational executives are in a much stronger position to respond proactively to international business challenges when they align business strategies, policies and behavior with cultural requirements.

Universal Competencies

At the same time, the best CEOs are able to focus on critical issues and alliances. They protect corporate interest and pursue business opportunities on a global scale. These CEOs use a range of leadership and communication competencies to focus their organization.

A key competency is building commitment among many stake-holders, including the board of directors, strategic partners and allies, institutional investors, employees, customers and national governments. Outstanding international CEOs are driven by a strong need to achieve, to continuously improve and compete against a standard of excellence. In some cases they are driven by a sense of social responsibility.

The Benefits of the Leadership Study

The results of this study had multifold uses which the multinational executives, managers or human resource leaders could derive. They could:

- Adapt their own behavior when operating in other cultures
- Recognize their own strengths and limitations
- Assess employees for different assignments according to their style and cultural adaptability
- Establish a system of leadership to select, develop, and retain adaptable multinational executives

The same findings will also help multinational executives, in:

1. Choosing the Right People

The complexities of the international marketplace make it increasingly difficult to maintain right control from a single corporate location. This is pushing many CEOs toward a leadership style that stresses participatory decision-making and implementation. They are placing much greater emphasis on choosing the right executives for the problem, tasks or situation and then empowering them to define what needs to be done and how to do it. Businesses will be able to use our finding to develop a systematic approach to selection.

This system of leadership includes planning for succession. A succession planning model for multinational executives is provided in the following section.

2. Managing International Alliances

Furthermore, our study will help executives manage strategic international alliances. While most of the CEOs in our study operate in their home countries, they increasingly sell to or collaborate with companies in other countries or regions of the world. How do they manage and sustain these partnerships?

Certainly, building a flexible infrastructure spanning multiple countries is one way. National and international companies are using computer based production, information and communication technologies to collaborate with strategic partners.

But a second factor is often missing: the appropriate competencies for managing international alliances. Our framework will guide executives as they adapt to each situation individually. In managing an international alliance an executive may use our finding to answer such questions as:

- How does my business partner want to build a relationship?
- How much planning does this management team need before moving forward?
- Which style of leadership will work best in our subsidiary in Asia? Who is the best match for that position?

Succession Planning for Multinational Executives

Talented multinational executives are vital for sustaining growth, but the companies that endure are the ones that have a strong system of leadership. Succession planning is a key element of any successful system of leadership.

Effective succession planning allows a company to retain its best multinational executives. They have a personal stake in the company's success because their personal development is wedded to the company's future. Succession planning also allows management to cull the organization of people who do not benefit the company or themselves.

Hay/McBer offers a six-step process for multinational executive succession planning:

Step 1: Strategic Review
Succession planning starts with a full review of the organization's strategic direction. Matching individuals to opportunities required a clear understanding of the market opportunities that successful leadership must target and exploit.

Step 2: Incumbent Analysis
Hay/McBer interviews incumbent executives to understand the current level of competence in the executive ranks. These incumbents are then benchmarked against the Hay/McBer executive database.

Step 3: Feeder Position Assessment
Hay McBer examines the jobs that feed executive positions, both functional and cross-functional. The skills, knowledge and competencies a person is likely to acquire by handling such feeder positions well are specified.

Step 4: Succession Plan
Next, Hay/McBer matches individual to key feeder positions by identifying vacancies or poorly filled positions and then developing plans for internal promotions or external recruitment.

Step 5: Development Plan
To close the gap between job requirements and personal competencies, Hay/McBer establishes a development plan for training and job rotation. Development needs may occur in two areas:

- Skill and Knowledge
- Key underlying characteristics of individuals

Step 6: Implementation
The organization is now ready to implement its succession plan both individually and company-wide.

International Adaptability

Hay/McBer concluded that the very best CEOs adapt their leadership style and organization policies and practices to the region or country where they are operating. As superior CEOs make complex choices about the future, they identity and use competencies critical for business success in a foreign market.

International Adaptability Continuums

The ability of CEOs to adapt their leadership style to cultural requirements is evident in their assumptions about:

1. Building business relationships
2. Choosing a basis for action
3. Exercising authority and leadership

For each dimension, the leadership study identified a continuum of business styles or management orientations, driven by cultural forces. Hay/McBer calls this framework 'International adaptability Continuums'.

These continuums allow a multinational executive to understand which adaptations and competencies are essential for success in a given part of the world. Executives increasingly operate in several cultures at once and conduct negotiations on a global scale. Their success depends on their ability to manage their own underlying cultural assumptions. The best executives are able to choose and control cultural orientation. They are flexible, moving along each continuum to select a management style appropriate for each international situation.

Continuum 1: Building Business Relationships— Personal Versus Contractual

This continuum reflects the manner in which an executive develops business relationships with strategic partners, suppliers, customers, government officials and others.

Personal Relationships: 'Trust and Mutual Respect are Essential'

At the Personal Relationship end of the continuum, the personal connections come first and play a major role in shaping the business relationships. Executives who follow this strategy tend to conduct business through the gradual development of trust and mutual respect.

Once they establish a personal link, these executives move on to other decisions, such as the terms of the deal. Since and individual connection is expected to last for many years, short-term financial gain may be less important than the health of the personal relationship.

Another characteristic of conducting business through the development of mutual respect and trust is what we call 'managing face'. These individuals demonstrate, through manners, symbols of office, speech patterns and actions that they are acting with authority. They show, in similar ways, that they respect the authority, position and age of their counter-parts.

Personal relationship building is particularly strong in the Far East and, to a lesser degree, in Europe. Even among North American CEOs, the importance of individual relationships appears to be growing.

To succeed in cultures that emphasize personal relationships, multinational executives need to develop two specific competencies: Developing Mutual Respect and Building Relationships.

Contractual Relationships: 'The Deal's the Thing'

Some cultures tend to subordinate personal relationship to a more explicit, and less flexible, contractual relationship. These executives make decisions based on price, performance, quality and other supposedly objective criteria. Trusts should be established through the successful completion of contracts. People are essentially equal and should all be treated in the same way. Contracts can and will be enforced.

CEOs forming contractual relationship tend to:

- Separate personal feelings from business merits. This executive will choose the best deal or take the lowest bid regardless of personal factors.

- Choose partners, suppliers, and other business connections based on performance rather than status. Such considerations as gender or ethnic background are immaterial-indeed, in some places, illegal.

In a culture that values contractual above personal relationships, a CEO must understand the competency of Objectivity. An individual with this competency attempts to see things clearly and does not let subjective feelings get in the way.

Continuum 2: Basis for Action— Planning versus Implementation

The Building Business Relationships continuum differentiates the cultural styles of personal and contractual relationships. For the second continuum, the CEO study found two opposing cultural styles for carrying out actions: Planning versus Implementations.

Executives obviously plan and implement actions in all parts of the world. Differences occur, however, in the relative weight given to each aspect of an action and the approach to the planning process.

Planning: 'Get the Right Plan'

At the planning end of the continuum, executives determine—in advance—exactly how the work will get done. The goal of this management style is to develop a detailed and rational plan and then present it so clearly that any reasonable employee will be able to carry it out.

All of the countries included in this study, except the US, were strong at the planning end of Continuum 2.

Implementation: 'Just Do It'

At the implementation end of the continuum, CEOs focus primarily on choosing the right people to carry out their plans. The key to this orientation is a careful assessment of the individuals involved. These executives place great trust in a chosen individual's ability to improvise in order to achieve a goal. The implementation style is characterized by a sense of urgency and is most effective in unstable and fast-changing environments. North American executives were stronger than their European and Asian counterparts in these qualities.

In our study, CEOs exhibited their implementation styles in a range of behaviors from the individualist acting alone to the more team-oriented leader who executes plans through other people.

Two competencies are needed to succeed in an implementation-oriented culture: *good judgment of people* and *personal initiative*.

Good Judgment of People
Most high-level initiatives are far too complex for the executive to complete alone. The ability to assess individual potential accurately is critical to the implementation cultural style. The willingness to trust and support carefully chosen subordinates is also essential.

Personal Initiative
Equally important in an implementation environment is Personal Initiative. People with initiative are eager to take action. They don't just think about the future; they act. Animosity toward bureaucratic structures is often an accompanying trait.

Continuum 3: Exercising Authority—Centralized Authority Versus Participatory Leadership

The basis for the Action Continuum differentiates the cultural styles of implementation and Planning. For the third continuum, the CEO study found two opposing cultural styles for exercising authority: Centralized Authority versus Participatory Leadership. All successful executives use their authority to obtain team commitment and co-operation. However, how they do this varies from country to country and between companies within countries.

Centralized Authority: 'I Lead Through Myself'
In a cultural environment of Centralized Authority, executives take a clear stance: they are the leaders and the decision makers in relation to their subordinates.

These CEOs describe and promote a vision which is essentially their own. They may acknowledge other contributions, but they still refer to it as 'my vision my idea' taking sole responsibility for the final decision to proceed. They excel at selling their vision to both their employees and to their board of directors. Often, they see themselves as having to overcome resistance to their ideas.

US and Mexican executives exhibit the centralized leadership style less often than their European, Canadian and Far Eastern counterparts.

Participatory Leadership: 'I Lead Through Others'

On the other hand, executives who excel at Participatory Leadership have a more subtle way of exercising authority. They begin by establishing a structure and process that allows teams to make collective decisions.

Although these leaders may disclaim responsibility for decisions, their role in facilitating and empowering the group is critical. Equally important is providing closure: articulating the decision and moving the group to the next phase.

Successful managers working in a participatory leadership environment demonstrate the Participatory Leadership competency. The manager solicits inputs and the team develops a vision. Team members are committed to their vision because they participated in its creation.

North American executives, particularly in the US, practice a participative leadership style that emphasizes teamwork.

Universal Competencies

While Hay/McBer discovered significant cultural differences in leadership styles, our researchers also identified a common set of cross-cultural competencies. Outstanding international CEOs adapt their behavior to the region or country where they operate. At the same time, all of them share Universal Competencies that transcend national boundaries. Successful executives modify the Universal Competencies for each culture they encounter.

Universal Competencies fall into three distinct clusters:

1. Sharpening the Focus
2. Building Commitment
3. Driving for Success

To determine those competencies that distinguish superior international CEO performance from average performance, we compared our study group of CEOs to Hay/McBer's database of 150 similar executives (the latter group does not have international responsibilities).

Cluster 1: Sharpening the Focus

The best executives are able to cut through a barrage of data and pinpoint the issues most important to their company. Their goals are to protect corporate interests from external threats and to pursue business opportunities that positively affect their organization. The Sharpening the Focus cluster includes four competencies:

1. Broad Scanning
Searching for knowledge about people, issues and events. These executives maintain sources of information on political, economic, technological and other developments outside the normal boundaries of their business.

2. Analytical Thinking
Understanding a situation by breaking it apart into smaller pieces or tracing the implications in a logical way. Executives with this competency make comparisons, set priorities and identify time sequences causal relationships or if-then relationships.

3. Conceptual Thinking
Identifying patterns, underlying issues or connections between situations that are not obviously related. These executives use creative, conceptual or inductive reasoning. Our study found that outstanding international CEOs combine Conceptual Thinking with Analytical Thinking to solve business problems.

4. Decisive Insight
Integrating Broad Scanning with Conceptual and Analytical Thinking. This combination produces both an insightful analysis and the precise identification of necessary actions. The result is a clear focus in providing direction for the organization.

The CEO of a European consumer conglomerate used his Sharpening the Focus competencies to give market direction to his company. First he described Broad Scanning:

My main role is to see everything ahead of time, like the frozen dinners line meant for today's thrifty customers who will agree to pay the added value on a product as long as it does not exceed a certain level. I can explain to my associates that, in some cases, we do not follow market trends. Products have to be analyzed again and modified when necessary. It's just something I feel, because I participate in seminars and have personal contacts that my associates do not have.

Then he gave an example of 'conceptual thinking':

To give you a specific example, I developed the 'clip' principle: when the differential between our price and the base price [of the generic product categories in the market] increases we face a higher risk of market share loss.

Next came the example of 'analytical thinking':

It's a very sensitive system that had to be demonstrated several times with tables showing price differentials: first the prices increase; then across the market share curve. 25 products were analyzed and the same trend was found in all cases: when differentials decreased, the market share simply increased.

The result was 'decisive insight':

Actually, I guessed a trend that nobody had seen so far. A product head might have perceived the trend somewhere but did not adopt a systematic approach and analyze the 25 products. When I found out how the market was developing, I warned them and asked them to reduce the differentials that were too wide.

The competencies in the 'Sharpening the Focus' cluster produce innovative ideas and a clear direction. They enable executives to focus people's commitment and enthusiasm.

Cluster 2: Building Commitment

Once they understand the critical issues affecting a situation, the best executives communicate a clear sense of direction. They are aware that cultural considerations heavily influence their employees' sense of responsibility and are able to build commitment among diverse coalitions.

There are four competencies in the Building Commitment Cluster:

1. Organizational Know-how
Understanding the organization and knowing who to influence. Outstanding executives create a vision and are able to gain commitment by understanding people's underlying attitudes, strengths and weaknesses.

2. Good Judgment of People
Choosing the right person for the job. Thirty-nine percent of international CEOs, most of them in the US, exhibit this competency.

3. Leadership
Creating group cooperation and commitment. Leadership may be exercised in either a participatory or centralized style (see 'exercising authority' dimension). But in either case, the effective executive aligns people's energy to focus on critical business objectives. Sixty-one percent of the international CEOs demonstrated leadership in a centralized leadership fashion.

4. Impact and Influence
Knowing how to persuade, convince or influence others to support an agenda. International CEOs demonstrate this competency considerably more often than the executives in the comparison sample.

Cluster 3: Driving for Success

Executives who are highly motivated to succeed are driven by four competencies:

1. Need to Achieve
Exhibiting a high motivation to succeed. Successful executives compete against an internal standard of excellence. Their need to achieve appears most often as:

- Taking initiative for improving performance
- Setting challenging but achievable goals

- Taking calculated entrepreneurial risks for the organization such as launching a new product or entering a competitive new market.

2. Self-confidence

Having the courage of their convictions even in the presence of uncertainty and ambiguity. These executives trust their judgment and do not give up in the face of challenges. Seventy-three percent of international CEOs had this competency; so did a similarly high percentage in the comparison group.

Self-confident leaders demonstrate courage of their convictions despite a high level of ambiguity in their work life. They do not give up when confronted with failure. As one CEO and chairman of the board of a federally owned European bank said:

> There's a quote from an American president saying, 'One man with a conviction has the majority.' I was just convinced that the way in which this business was run was wrong. And I was able to communicate that (to the board), so I gained their support.

Successful CEOs also trust their inclinations even when they don't have all the answers. One North American executive, responsible for the introduction of a new consumer product illustrated this point when he recalled:

> Our research said the new product was good, but I just wasn't satisfied. I told him, I'm going into this test market but you and I both know we can make a better product, and you have to keep working on this. I want a great product.

3. Social Responsibility

Perceiving their role as extending beyond the confines of their organization; using their power and influence for positive change in society, many of the CEOs in this study spontaneously mentioned this kind of responsibility in their interviews.

As one CEO reflected:

> For me, personally, the greatest challenge is to keep the company moving dynamically in all the new markets and make sure that profitability and cash flow are sufficient. At the same time, we can invest in environmental measures. We should be able to say, in ten years' time, that we

have become, in large measure, self sufficient and no longer inflict damage on nature or cause problems in the world.

4. Initiating Action

Taking action now to create opportunities or prevent problems in the future. The executive's 'drive for success' impacts the company when the executive Initiates Action. This action is driven by a long-term view (more than one year away).

We found that successful international CEOs are able to integrate the three clusters of 'sharpening the focus', 'building commitment', and 'driving for success'. These executives exhibit a higher level of continuous learning, satisfaction and self-confidence.

While an executive must possess an array of universal competencies in order to 'play the game', the ability to adapt leadership styles across cultures determines whether the executive will 'win the game'.

In the final analysis, then, how do you master global leadership? The answer is complex. Executives must individually make the right choices that will keep their organization focused, yet capable of adapting quickly to intensifying global competition.

Conclusion: Mastering Global Leadership

Our study establishes a framework for identifying how executives must adapt. Furthermore, it analyzes the competencies necessary for multinational leadership. Executives can use our framework to develop an understanding of their foreign business counterparts and how they operate.

Executives who conduct business locally require little conscious adaptation beyond their national borders. However, as their companies grow, so does the need to interact with international businesses and cultures. Most of the CEOs in our study led local organizations whose survival increasingly depends on the ability to conduct business internationally.

Executives who operate internationally must be aware of, and in control of, their own cultural assumptions about how to conduct business. They can no longer afford to accept without question their home culture's view of the world. The ability to move back and forth along the International Adaptability continuums is crucial to sustained success in global markets.

In making choices, executives must be careful not to cross the fine line between generalizing and stereotyping a culture. In some cases, a company's corporate culture may not conform to the prevailing assumptions for doing business in its home country. German business culture, for example, is often viewed as planning oriented and centralized. One leading German software manufacturer, however, operates with a highly entrepreneurial and decentralized corporate culture. Simply assuming that this German firm functions according to national norm would be a serious error of judgment.

Adapting one's own behavior to the individual situation is the executive's first step to success. The second is the ability to choose the right person for the right job in an international setting. Executives who manage multinational businesses must be able to select people who can identify and, adapt to, business requirements in a specific country.

The most successful international postings match a person's style to local requirements.

Many international companies try to hire locally for key leadership positions. While local mangers may clearly understand cultural assumptions for doing business locally, they may lack some of the universal competencies critical for effective management on an international scale. It is the task of the multinational executive to ensure that the local manager develops the three critical Universal Competencies: Sharpening the Focus, Building Commitment, and Driving for Success.

Mastering the Two Dimensions of Global Leadership

The key to global leadership is to master both dimensions of leadership. Successful international executives must be able to adapt their business style to other parts of the world. They must also, acquire and practice the Universal Competencies. Together, these qualities will lead their organization to international success.

About the Authors

SIGNE M. SPENCER is Senior Consultant at HayGroup, in the McClelland Center for Research and Innovation. A graduate in psychology from the University of Chicago, she also studied M.Ed. in Human Development and Psychology from Harvard.

At HayGroup, Ms Spencer has worked with clients such as IBM, Tyco, Standard and Poors, BAE Systems, Catholic Health Association, Huawei, Singapore Ministry of Education, Novelis, PepsiCo, Seton Hospitals, Delphi, and many others, developing leadership competency models, a range of implementation strategies and high-stakes assessments. Her work has included all aspects of competency research, including integrating competency findings across a wide variety of jobs and improving methods of competency research, designing and validating competency applications, and providing individual feedback and coaching to executives. In addition, she designs interactive on-line tutorials to teach HayGroup's motivational and managerial concepts and to facilitate competency development.

She is co-author of *Competency Assessment Methods* (1992) and *Competence at Work* (1993).

THARUMA RAJAH is an International Partner and Regional Director for HayGroup Asia, and is based in Kuala Lumpur, Malaysia.

He leads the effort in Asia to develop HayGroup's Leadership and Talent Management Practice; train and develop a multidisciplinary consulting team, and integrate and augment local skills and knowledge with HayGroup's worldwide network of over 88 offices in 43 countries. Tharuma has consulted across a whole spectrum of industries ranging from education, finance, telecommunications, manufacturing, oil and gas, FMCG, and the public sector. He has extensive international consulting experience across most countries in the Asia-Pacific and related MNC client engagements in the Middle East and Africa, UK and the US.

Tharuma works around helping organizations make the major shift required for organizational transformation by providing insights to clients about the scale of change facing them, and thus mitigate their risk of derailment on that journey. He helps them develop and implement talent and leadership transformation interventions, and clarifies the impact of business change on organizations and roles. He is also Executive Coach to many Fortune 500 business leaders in Asia.

Tharuma joined HayGroup in 1993 after 11 years with National Semiconductor, a Silicon Valley-based American Electronics MNC, and has extensive experience in manufacturing, human resources and TQM functions.

He holds a Bachelor of Law degree from the University of London and has been called to the Bar of England and Wales. He is a Member of The Honorable Society of Lincoln's Inn, United Kingdom.

S.A. NARAYAN is Director, Human Resources, at Bharat Petroleum Corporation Limited. A graduate in science and law from Bombay University, he specialized in Personnel Management at the Tata Institute of Social Sciences in Mumbai. He is a member of the National Institute of Personnel Management and National HRD Network. He is a member of HR Committee of ASSOCHAM (Association Chamber of Commerce and Industry), New Delhi and the Academic Council of University of Petroleum and Energy Studies, Dehradun.

He has over 33 years of work experience in HR, during which time his work has covered the entire gamut of HR practices in a large *Fortune* 500 company like BPCL. He oversees all people related policies and practices for over 14,000 employees of the Company. Besides, as a member of the Board of BPCL and two other Joint Ventures/Subsidiaries, he has in-depth knowledge of the overall workings of these companies and as well of the oil Industry.

SEETHARAMAN MOHAN is Executive Director, Human Resources, at Bharat Petroleum Corporation Limited. He is a mechanical engineering graduate from the Birla Institute of Technology & Science, Pilani, and MBA from the Indian Institute of Management in Bangalore.

Mr Mohan was trained in UK as a 'Trainer' in 'Change Management' at the Stanford University and has attended an Executive Development Programme at Kellogg. He has spoken at several international conferences in the UK, USA, Singapore and South East Asia. His work has included developing corporate strategies for attracting and retaining talent and implementing support systems to bring about a sharp focus on performance. Currently he is working on Talent Management process for BPCL. He is a member of the Executive Committee of Bombay Management Association (BMA) and Chairman of the Management Development Programme Committee of BMA. He is also a member of the Institution of Engineers as well as a member of the HRD-IR Committee of the Bombay Chamber of Commerce & Industry and Corporate Governance Committee of Indian Merchant Chamber. He is currently working on his Ph.D.

GAURAV LAHIRI is Director, Strategic Clients, at HayGroup, London. A mathematics graduate from the Delhi University, he specialized in Human Resources and Business Strategy at the Xaviers Labour Relations Institute in Jamshedpur.

He joined HayGroup in 2000 and works with clients to align their organizations with their strategic agenda—including decoding strategies, designing organization structures, implementing talent management programmes and formulating reward strategies to drive performance and motivation. Gaurav's specialization is in Organization Effectiveness. He has helped his clients reorganize based on their strategies, re-engineered their processes to help save costs and worked with the executive teams to align their aspirations. He has also helped his clients research and develop competency models for outstanding performance. He managed a seminal global research project on identifying the competencies of an Indian CEO. Gaurav is also an experienced job evaluator and has conducted work measurement studies in several countries in Asia Pacific across various sectors.

Gaurav has authored several papers on Post Merger Integration, Change Management and has won several prizes and awards, including the McKinsey Best Management Paper of the year in 1999.